T0061816

Flight from Afghanistan

Flight from
Afghanistan
Tella's Story

Tella Omeri

Whittles Publishing

Published by

Whittles Publishing Ltd.,
Dunbeath,
Caithness, KW6 6EG,
Scotland, UK
www.whittlespublishing.com

Printed and bound in Great Britain by
Severn, Gloucester

ISBN 978-184995-434-1

© 2021 Tella Omeri

*All rights reserved.
No part of this publication may be reproduced,
stored in a retrieval system, or transmitted,
in any form or by any means, electronic,
mechanical, recording or otherwise
without prior permission of the publishers.*

Contents

In clear and utterly compelling English, this moving memoir tells the story of the agony, and the ecstasy, of one refugee - and of every refugee. A must read for anyone interested in the triumph of Afghanistan's spirit over its seemingly endless suffering, and in the universal plight of those forced by conflict to flee their homeland.

Sir Sherard Cowper-Coles, British Ambassador to Afghanistan 2007-10

"Afghan refugees represent one of the world's largest protracted refugee populations. Over the past four decades, many have been forced from their homes to never see them again. Some were able to return, for a while, but had their lives upended by a fresh eruption of conflict and violence – either to be displaced elsewhere in the country, or to become refugees yet again." – *Amnesty International*

Introduction

I have written this short story not for any sympathy, but by way of explanation as to what drives someone like me to run away from my own country regardless of the dangers and to seek sanctuary in a foreign land where some may say I have no right to live.

I hope also that it will give readers an insight into what has happened over the years in my home country, Afghanistan, which, through no fault of its native inhabitants, has been invaded and brutalised by successive regimes and outsiders. Some have tried to come to our aid but, through lack of understanding or perhaps for other more sinister motives, have only succeeded in making matters worse.

International leaders continue to pick over our bones, trying to reach peace agreements to bring an end to the fighting which has been raging for decades and for too long it went unnoticed by most media outlets, but somehow failing to recognise the wishes of Afghans, who represent the second largest refugee group in the world.

I have a third reason for writing this story and it is to try and persuade people that Muslims are not universally evil and Islam is not a religion to be feared. There are certainly those who manipulate the teachings of the Koran for their own ends spreading misinformation through various media channels, but that is not the true faith. Despite what President Trump said, Islam does not hate the West. Equally, despite what the likes of the Islamic State group and extremist preachers proclaim, they are doing more harm to fellow Muslims than Christians. Afghans are bombed and attacked by all sides and when it becomes too much those who survive either take up arms themselves or flee.

When you run away from your home country with little or no money, you place yourself in the hands of complete strangers whom you have to trust, sometimes with your very life. These are the human traffickers operating around the world in plain sight – if you know where to look. They don't care if you are male or female, young or old, pregnant or not and certainly don't care if you live or die because it is simply business to them and they thrive because political leaders cannot resolve their differences.

Refugees, who are not the same as economic migrants, don't want to flee; they are forced to run from the bullets and the bombs. They would much rather remain in their homeland even if life is hard, where economies are underdeveloped and where there is no possibility of anything changing for the better in their lifetime. The point is it is home, for all its faults.

If you are lucky you will reach the safety of a country where, as a refugee, you are offered shelter, but that is no guarantee of a secure life. Others who made it before you have established businesses and are perfectly willing to exploit the vulnerable new arrivals that are naturally drawn to their own kind. When you buy your pizza or receive your home delivery be aware of the individual serving you. They will be working long hours, for little if any pay and in many cases will be living in dirty, overcrowded conditions exploited by unscrupulous landlords as much as the human traffickers exploited them.

So what, you may ask. They are probably illegal immigrants, not paying taxes and living off the state – they deserve everything they get. I arrived in the UK illegally but the day after I was arrested and threw myself on the mercy of the courts and the generosity of the people I met, I immediately went in search of work.

Despite what I went through I consider myself fortunate. I have been granted British citizenship and my children are receiving a wonderful education, something I never enjoyed, but every day I think of home. There, children attend schools where they preach hatred and violence, the religious leaders encourage *jihad* while the politicians seem incapable of winning the peace which the ordinary people long for and deserve.

If you have nothing and a charismatic figure offers you money to take up arms to fight in a struggle you know little about, you will be tempted, as members of my own family were. It is justified as patriotism to drive out the infidel, but there are no winners in this struggle. In recent history Afghanistan has witnessed civil wars, invasions, assassinations of political leaders, a staggering growth in the cultivation of cannabis and heroin and an increasing exodus of refugees seeking a better life. They know that they won't always be accepted, that they will always be foreigners in a foreign land despite what it may say on their shiny new passports, but it is better than the constant threat of bombardment from the air, kidnap, rape and murder on the ground and the certain knowledge that any peace agreement will be short-lived because your country is too strategically important to be left alone.

No one wants to be a refugee or live in a camp without warmth or running water, or risk their lives clinging to the sides of a crowded boat or the underside of a fast-moving lorry, but if the alternative is certain death at the point of a bayonet then it is worth taking a chance.

Tella Omeri

ONE

Life under Russian control

I was born on 1 January 1979 in Kushgumbad near the provincial capital, Jalalabad, in eastern Afghanistan, which is not remarkable as everyone in my village was said to be born on New Year's Day. Babies were delivered at home because we had no hospitals, doctors or midwives so no one kept a proper record or issued birth certificates. No one could remember the precise day or even the month I arrived so in time I chose 1 January as my birthday – it seemed easier to remember. But my mom said I was an "unlucky child" as I was born the same year the Soviet Union invaded Afghanistan; perhaps she was right because before long they had destroyed my home and virtually my entire village.

The communists had seized power in the country under President Nur Mohammad Taraki in 1978 and immediately began redistributing the land among their supporters. Taraki locked up his opponents, and villagers who complained about the loss of their land were executed. His dictatorship style of government didn't last long, however, as he himself was murdered on 8 October 1979 prompting the Soviet invasion on Christmas Eve.

The first sounds I recall hearing were of bombs going off in the mountains of the Hindu Kush as the Russians attacked rebel positions, but for a child growing up in Kushgumbad none of this fighting had any impact at first; the bombing may even have been a source of excitement, like a distant fireworks display.

Everyone calls me simply "Tella" as most Afghans are known by one name. It means gold in Farsi. It was only when I came to the UK that I realised that people had first names and surnames so, being a Muslim, I decided to call myself Tella Mohammad as, of course, I had no birth certificate to say otherwise. I didn't realise that we have connections with Arab settlers who came to our village in the distant past and some villagers actually referred to us as 'Arabs'. I found out later that my real surname should be Omeri as my grandfather who was a big tribal leader in his day was called Omeri Khan. Now all my cousins in America and the UK use Omeri as their surname which I have also decided is the correct and wise thing to do. In today's world to be called Mohammad invites comments and even accusations of being a terrorist which is not fair on children who cannot answer back or even understand. I told my own daughter when she started school in the UK not to worry if her classmates teased her saying she must be a terrorist and made comments about women wearing burqas, and just to concentrate on her studies because the other children knew no better.

Our village lies between Jalalabad Airport and the Kabul River. When I lived there it had about a hundred homes, a shop and our house was at the end of a long line looking down the street towards the main mosque on the other side of a stream. It was a simple construction made of mats and dried mud bricks with wooden beams and a staircase outside leading up to the roof. In the hot summer nights we would sleep on the roof and watch the Soviet gunships fly overhead to Jalalabad Airport about two kilometres away. I remember I could even see the pilots' faces and would wave to them, although I don't think they waved back. The house was big enough for our family and my father's four brothers and their wives to live together. To protect ourselves from thieves, who came from neighbouring villages, like most houses we had a heavy wooden gate, which I was not strong enough to push open. Petty crime was normal, but I think they came in search of food – it was more to do with survival than getting rich.

My father, Ghulam Hazrat, was a farmer and kept some sheep, two big cows, two horses and sometimes hired a donkey. He owned some land and, in local terms, I suppose we were better off than many. When I was considered old enough, aged four, my mom would wake me early after milking the cows to carry a bucket of fresh milk to my aunt, who didn't keep animals, but lived in a neighbouring village called Qali Malik, a 20-minute walk away for me, while my father attended morning prayers in the mosque. Then we would sit down together and have some green tea with sugar and bread for our breakfast. I never got used to having milk in my tea because I could see the cows and the dirt around them. Sometimes, if we were lucky, my mom would cook *paratha* which is a flatbread with some oil. We ate mostly vegetables and occasionally meat once a week; chicken was very expensive so it was a rare treat when my father brought one home.

After breakfast my father would take me out into the fields with a shovel to help him work on the land and plant seeds for the vegetables – tomatoes and cucumbers. We would also go fishing in the Kabul River, which today has flooded much of the land because nobody tended the banks and streams. Every day we would bring back three or four fish; sometimes the fish were so big my father could not carry them home, but what we didn't need for ourselves we cut up and shared with the other villagers because no one had a fridge to keep the food fresh.

The village had no electricity or running water. The women would walk down to the river each morning and carry containers of water back home on their heads. In the summer men would bring blocks of ice from Jalalabad which would be cut up to cool our drinks. In fact we could have had electricity when the Russians first offered it, but the tribal elder said he would be blamed if a child stuck their finger in a socket, was electrocuted and died. He rejected the offer and being the elder no one could argue with the decision so we continued to use oil lamps. Rising early with the sun and going to bed when it got dark had its benefits as everyone seemed to have good eyesight and no one wore glasses in those days.

Once I had finished in the fields my mom would teach me the Koran and how to pray. I never went to school nor did most of the other children my age, although some of the older boys went to school in Jalalabad. When I had finished my studies I was free to go and play with the other children with sticks and stones making up our own imaginary games. It was a simple childhood but we never seemed to want for anything that I was aware of. I had one pair of shoes, although most of the time

I went barefoot, and two changes of clothes even though we could have afforded more but my parents did not seem to worry about such things; instead all the villagers cared for one another and shared what little we had.

One of my uncles had a wooden Philips radio with four big batteries at the back. People would come and listen to the news more in amazement at a human voice coming out of a box than for any other reason. Slowly people began buying tape recorders and started listening to Afghan music and increasingly people had musicians at their wedding parties dancing to live music. My father must have been one of the first to invite an Afghan performer to sing at his wedding.

Afghanistan is a multi-ethnic and multi-tribal society – 14 different ethnic groups are mentioned in its national anthem. The best known are probably the Pashtuns, Tajiks and Hazara. The Pashtuns are in the majority and dominate political life while the Tajiks and Hazara tend to stay in the cities – the Hazara, who hail from the Mongol people, usually do most of the heavy labour and street cleaning, so even in Afghan society there is a pecking order, which is the same the world over.

My father was Pashtun while my mom is Tajik but her ancestors were Persian. Our village was a mixture of ethnic groups although most of the villagers spoke Farsi when I was a child even though we were in a Pashtun area; when my mom speaks Pashto I can tell when she makes mistakes. Despite this mix of tribal people we used to travel to other villages for parties and weddings and everyone seemed to get along. In time my gift for languages as well as my appearance, a mix of Afghan and Persian, would be crucial in my escape from Afghanistan.

When he was not working the land, my father was something of a travelling salesman crossing the border into Pakistan to trade – there were no passports – taking dried fruit and Afghan carpets, which were popular in Peshawar, in exchange for exotic perfumes from India which he would sell in Jalalabad. Another lucrative sideline which some villagers had was selling the cannabis growing in our fields to the Russians in Jalalabad Airport in exchange for aviation fuel which in turn would be sold in the city. During the Russian occupation cannabis production grew rapidly and since the Americans arrived in 2001 it seems to have increased even more dramatically. We all had our suspicions that the US army was somehow involved and, of course, I cannot prove it, but I wonder why they have such an interest in Helmand Province and the town of Sangin because that is the heart of all cannabis production today. The drugs trade in Afghanistan is booming, regardless of who is in power, producing four-fifths of the world's opium. Efforts to persuade farmers to grow wheat instead of poppy failed as they simply started irrigating and cultivating desert land to produce bumper harvests, today using solar panels to help pump water to irrigate their expanding crops.

On my father's return from one of his trips, he learned he was engaged to be married when his friends came up to congratulate him. He apparently looked surprised and asked if she was at least beautiful. My grandmother told him not to worry as they had chosen the better looking of two daughters, not the "difficult" one who later married one of my uncles. My father told me that he didn't choose my mom; it was an arranged marriage which was the custom and tradition. Happily it was a strong marriage and eventually, as can happen, they grew to like and, I hope, love one another.

For a time my father and many other villagers also worked in an olive factory the Russians had built in Jalalabad when Taraki was in power, and he would always bring home a jar of olives which was another treat. But the first sign of trouble that I was aware of was when someone dropped a piece of metal in the machinery sabotaging the plant which never reopened. It may have stopped the factory working, but it also stopped many Afghans making a little extra money. I don't know if this was the first time I heard of the Mujahideen, which simply means fighter for the Muslim faith, but it would certainly have angered my father who was not a supporter of many of their tactics. Some would keep their prisoners captive only releasing them if they agreed to leave the Afghan army and others would cut their throats. The Soviet occupation was a brutal time. There are well-documented accounts of Russian helicopters landing in fields and abducting women they found, flying away with them and raping them so they were dishonoured in their families' eyes. The secret police KhAD – Khadamat-e Aetla'at-e Dawlati (Secret Intelligence Agency) – adopted similar tactics in the cities stopping young women at random and abducting them.

As a child I often played with my friends near the river and sometimes we could see the Mujahideen wading across with their rifles held above the heads. We would sit next to them no doubt admiring their guns like all little boys, commenting on their long beards and they would be so friendly, but all the time they would be looking warily up at the Soviet helicopters flying overhead. They would ask us about our families and what our fathers did. I would innocently point to my father working in the fields and say that he was a farmer. I later realised, of course, that what they really wanted to know was if my father was in the Communist Afghan army. They would then go and talk to the elders trying to convince them to send their children to join the fight against the Russians, join the *jihad*. They would say that Afghanistan is our land and the Koran teaches that if someone occupies your land you must fight and if you die you will go to paradise and have many virgins. As I was still only a child I was safe from this at least.

They tried to convince more and more people to help them and if anyone didn't have sons then they said that they must have money, food or warm clothes to give. I remember my mom giving them three or four flatbreads and fresh onions every time they came, but she had no choice as they would be carrying guns saying it was our duty to help. She and other villagers would help them out of fear while others revealed that some communist supporters were living in their villages. If people resisted they might be accused of being communists themselves or communist sympathisers and would be killed; the outcome was a country where no one felt safe from the invaders or even from betrayal by their own people.

But not everyone agreed with the Russians' portrayal of the Mujahideen as being rebels. Some villagers didn't call them Mujahideen; they called them *Ashrar*, which is a Farsi word for troublemakers. My father never called them Mujahideen; he somehow knew that in the end the innocent would always pay the price.

Some people from our village joined the Afghan army but it was more of a career to serve their country and earn some money rather than out of loyalty to the Soviets and they were careful to stay in Jalalabad. My mom's brother was one of those who joined up and only on rare occasions came to our village. Once he arrived on a motorbike with a sidecar and gave me a ride. Needless to say, I was thrilled, completely oblivious to what the uniform or motorbike represented. He was not a communist at heart though and when the army became more pro-Soviet people he left and turned against it. My mom warned her brother never to come back on his motorbike again or she would kill him herself because the Mujahideen might think the village was sympathetic to the Soviet invaders. The Russians didn't really trust the Afghan recruits anyway saying that during the day you are our friends but at night you turn against us, which was true as attacks and sabotage continued throughout their occupation.

My father accused the Mujahideen of supporting the Americans who by then were supplying weapons including Stinger missiles to the Pakistani regime of General Zia al Haq who would then distribute some of them to the seven Mujahideen groups he favoured. These were all Sunni and were dubbed "the Peshawar Seven" when they later formed an alliance in 1988. Pakistan made money on the side for sure, but it also sowed division among the Afghan fighters and people. My father would say to his brothers that this was not Afghanistan's fight, we were not against Russia, and that we should simply let the Russians cross Afghanistan and go to India or Pakistan or to the Black Sea. The Mujahideen were killing innocent people because they didn't know who would die in the attacks they launched – maybe children walking near the airport or in the cities. He said the Mujahideen were destroying the country which was caught in the middle of a fight between America and Russia. He didn't actually say this to the Mujahideen because he was scared of them but he said it to his own brothers trying to persuade them not to join the Mujahideen, but they joined anyway. My younger uncle, Ghulam Haidar, became a leading commander with more than 100 men under his control. When the Russians eventually pulled out in 1989 he said *jihad* was over and he gave up fighting to become a teacher in our village. He is an old man today.

I asked him once what the difference was between Russia and America and he just laughed and said the Americans fooled us. When the Russians had gone he said America had just left us with terrorists. Those terrorists are today's Taliban, which means students of madrassas. Hollywood even made a film about the conflict called *Charlie Wilson's*

War which told the story of a US Congressman's efforts with CIA backing to help the Mujahideen fight the Soviet forces by sending arms shipments to the Mujahideen called Operation Cyclone. They succeeded in getting rid of the Russians but what have they left behind? A country with rival factions all armed with sophisticated weapons. And, of course, by 2019 it had trapped America in its longest war; after 18 years the USA was uncertain how to withdraw its own troops while maintaining the peace, although what Afghanistan faces could never be described as peace. Maybe America never wanted to leave entirely as social media is alive with stories of US forces smuggling valuable uranium out of the country from its bases in Helmand Province. Whatever the truth, Afghanistan is certainly rich in natural resources which make it attractive to outsiders, quite apart from its strategic geographical location.

Afghans have been used throughout history. In relatively modern times Great Britain was defeated in 1842 having failed to occupy Afghanistan as a defence against Soviet designs on India. Then the Mujahideen with US support via Pakistan drove out the Russian troops in February 1989, but Afghanistan has never been conquered nor has it harmed its neighbours. It was one of the hardest places for Islam to be introduced where multiple faiths were traditionally followed. But extremists from the Islamic State of Iraq and the Levant (ISIL) are now locked in their own struggle for domination with the Taliban, while the Afghan government launches attacks against their bases killing civilians in the process.

When I was growing up, the threat to villages like ours not only came from the differing Mujahideen groups who usually visited our village by night, but also from the Afghan army working for the Russians who came in their tanks by day. They would suddenly arrive and demand that young men should join them. There was no way to refuse so families like ours dug secret shelters to hide in whenever the army was approaching. Ours was big enough for three people to hide in and was dug in the ground near where we kept the animals knowing that the soldiers would not want to go into those dirty areas. This was normal life for our family and friends not only trying to make a living by growing what we could, but also resisting the competing demands of the Afghan army and Mujahideen.

However, until I was six it was a happy childhood. We didn't have much but we didn't need much. My parents must have been all too aware of the tensions, even the dangers, but for me it was a simple case of growing up in a close family of uncles and aunts. I played with the other children clearly unaware of any threats from the Mujahideen who were supposedly on our side because they were fellow Afghans, but wary every time the "foreigners", the Soviet soldiers, appeared. I didn't know that Afghans themselves were taking sides, some joining the Afghan army under Russian control, or even that the Mujahideen were themselves split; they may have been united in a common aim of driving out the Soviets just as they have always united against invaders, but not all were being equally supported by Pakistan. I do remember those times when my mom had to give food to the Mujahideen when they demanded help and I probably was aware of the anxiety at the time as my parents argued after they had gone. They were not angry with each other but they were angry with the way our village, and others, was being squeezed by both sides.

My landlocked country, I now clearly understand, sits in a difficult and dangerous position bordering six other countries but, as the world knows, for centuries it has been a battleground between East and West. The Afghan village people are not invited to peace talks; they are the pawns in a bigger political game and more often than not are what is dismissed as collateral damage. When I say I come from Afghanistan people say it is a bad country, but it is not. It is a country in which outsiders have tried and always failed to impose their wishes, their regimes and even their beliefs, but it is not a "bad country" and in my childish mind I must have divided up the very real dangers from the excitement.

On one occasion, as I watched the Mujahideen wading across the river, I wanted to tell them that they were in danger because Afghan soldiers were hiding ready to attack them. The army were right next to us where we were playing, so close we could even touch their AK47s but they warned us not to go to the river because we would be killed. They told us not to make a sound as they were looking for troublemakers, and they were just there to protect us. We thought it was wonderful they were going to protect us but when the Mujahideen were halfway across the river they started shooting at them. Some died and were carried away by the current; others managed to make it back to the other bank and disappeared into the bushes, but then the helicopters would fly low over the area and start shooting if they spotted any of them. I saw this maybe four or five times when I was still only five. It was like a terrible movie for me but it was real life. On any other day these same Mujahideen might have been in our homes asking for bread and warm clothing, but now they were being shot as someone else's enemy as I looked on. I don't know how my child's mind made sense of it all at the time; the killing became so normal, almost routine, that I just returned home, probably excitedly telling my parents what I had seen, and then carried on as though nothing had happened. No one spoke about trauma or anxiety, although what is happening now on a daily basis in Afghanistan's cities is more extreme and I worry constantly about my friends and family members I have left behind.

On another occasion I had been with my father working in the fields when he sent me to wash my face and hands in the river. He told me to be careful not to move any stones as there might have been snakes. When I got to the river and bent down over the water I noticed some hair and realised it was a body. I called my father to say that I had found something. It was in fact two men, one older man and a young man, their faces white and green as they must have been in the water a long time and they had been shot presumably by the Russians or Afghan army. I ran home full of excitement, possibly even pride, to tell my mother what I had found, not my father, then as no one recognised them our imam and the villagers all agreed that the bodies should be buried in our graveyard.

However, my family, indeed my entire village was about to become just another statistic in this struggle. I was now six and the fighting between the Mujahideen and the Soviet forces was becoming intense. While we may have thought we were safe from the worst of the fighting because we were so close to Jalalabad Airport and therefore too risky for the rebel fighters to launch attacks, it was only a matter of time before Kushgumbad became the front line for one fateful day. I don't know who I really blame the most for what was about to happen: our own Mujahideen, the Americans for arming them, Pakistan for its manipulation or the Russians for invading. All I do know is that for one family the fighting was about to have terrible consequences. It was no movie, rather a brutal introduction into what was already happening to the rest of our country.

TWO

Russian attack on village

In the summer of 1985, very early one morning, it must have been about three o'clock as it was still dark and everyone was asleep, five Mujahideen fighters came across the river and slipped into our village. They usually operated in small groups so they could not be easily seen from the air.

They were led by an infamous Mujahideen commander nicknamed *Marg*, which means death in Farsi. Although he was from a different area, he was well known to us as he came to our village many times and was always trying to launch attacks on Jalalabad airport, but until then never actually from Kushgumbad. One member of his family was in the Afghan army, another was in the Mujahideen and another, like my father, had nothing to do with either of them. So Marg was a wanted man and his regular visits to Kushgumbad, and the fact that one of our villagers was a leading Mujahideen commander, always made us vulnerable to Russian attention, although, precisely because we were so close to the airport and could to some extent be monitored by their security cameras, we had never been attacked by the Russians.

That night Marg and his men had obviously decided that they needed to get as close as possible to the airport and our village gave them the best vantage point so as not to miss when they fired their rockets at the helicopters. The noise woke everyone. I had seen rockets being fired in the past and I recognised the noise immediately as they raced through the air until they exploded on impact and, of course, I knew the sound of incoming rockets which would make us run and hide.

Standing on our rooftops we could see the fires burning at the airport. The attack had been successful but there was no cheering from us, I recall; instead probably a realisation among the elders about what would inevitably follow.

As soon as they fired their rockets the Mujahideen left the village without saying a word, crossing the river which made it difficult for any Russian tanks to follow, and disappeared into the night. The whole attack probably lasted no more than ten minutes as the fighters were limited by what they could carry. The impact for our family would last a lifetime.

I wasn't scared because I was used to the sound a rocket made and I never thought we would be killed because the attack had nothing to do with us – it was between the Mujahideen and the Russians. But the elders were angry because they could already see that families were slowly but surely abandoning the village as the fighting, the bombing and the killing were everywhere. One day five families might leave, another day maybe ten. They were all going to Pakistan or Iran and some even thought it would be safer in Jalalabad city.

And now the elders must have known that the Russians would retaliate even though there was nothing we could have done to stand up against the Mujahideen to prevent the village being used in this way because not only were we unarmed, but we also would have been accused of being communists.

For a time all was quiet and the village got back to its usual morning routine. My mom got on with her milking and my father got ready for early morning prayers in the mosque. No doubt everyone hoped that the attack on the airport would be blamed on rebel fighters and the search for them would continue elsewhere.

It was still quite dark, around 5am, when my father walked towards the mosque at the end of our street; in the gloom he could make out a group of four tanks and heavily armed soldiers. Very slowly he turned round and then ran to our secret hideout because he thought the Russians were again searching for men to join the army. Nobody believed the Russians would attack – at least not so soon – so my father didn't think to tell my mom not to make me take the morning milk to my aunt. It just seemed like any other day to my mom, who at that stage had not even seen the tanks, so she was happy to send me on my way, barefoot as usual, to my aunt.

As I passed the little shop at the end of the street I saw the tanks and 15 men from our village lined up against a wall by the stream with their hands tied behind their backs. As I turned the corner the soldiers opened fire from the rooftops and from the ground with AK47s shooting the men one by one. Some of the bullets ricocheted off the ground near my feet. One man who had already been hit in the ankle by a flying bullet jumped on top of me knocking me to the ground, spilling my milk, my ears ringing from the noise of gunfire. As he landed on top of me he broke my right arm but saved my life; I have been left-handed ever since. He assumed that he was going to die anyway but he thought at least he would save one child. He lay on top of me for no more than 20 or 30 seconds, and when he saw his chance he quickly dragged me into the shop, which typically for the poorest neighbourhoods was actually in someone's home. The shopkeeper was a very old man and he was crying but he told us to leave by a back door so we wouldn't be seen and I ran home.

The Russians had picked the men out at random, even pulling some from the mosque. One of them was actually in the Afghan army and tried to protest: "I am one of you guys, check my papers," I could hear him shouting. They ignored his plea saying he was working with the Mujahideen and now he would be punished. We don't trust you anymore, they said, and they shot him dead. The rest of the men said nothing because they thought they were just going to be taken away to join the army. But they shot every one of them. An elderly man came up and shouted at the soldiers had they no fear of God for what they had done, destroying the village community. Those were to be his last words. One of the gunmen shouted back at the old man: "Shut your mouth. If you shelter the Mujahideen you will see the same thing again and again" and they shot him in front of my eyes. They could easily have shot me but perhaps they thought I was just a small child and didn't bother although I could see the bullets bouncing off the ground next to me before I managed to escape.

The 15 men, aged about 25 or 30 years, were all innocent and had no connection with the Mujahideen, who may have had some secret contact in our village. They had simply made the mistake of coming outside when they heard the tanks arrive. The men who did the shooting were not Russians – we called them Sarter. They could not be frightened because they believed they had already sacrificed their lives to the army and were ready to die. They wore civilian clothes not uniforms – I suppose they were a bit like mercenaries. But the fact is they were Afghans killing other Afghans. Today the Taliban are killing other Afghans saying: "Why are you working with the Americans?" They say their imams and mullahs have told them that they are allowed to kill anyone who works with the Americans. At that time most of the priests were on the side of the Mujahideen, although the imam in our village had nothing to do with them because I knew him, although he certainly would have known people in the Mujahideen. But we paid him, giving him free food to teach us the Koran. We used to invite imams from different villages to visit and they could stay as long as they wanted. Most of them had connections with the Mujahideen but they all agreed and gave us permission to kill the Russians because they had occupied our country.

Everyone else was hiding in their homes not daring to come out until they saw the tanks moving away. The shooting lasted maybe just a few minutes, although it seemed longer. Then the imams, the wives and sisters came out and I could see the bullet wounds in the heads of the dead men, and the stream ran red with their blood. My mom was crying and shouting that they had killed two of her cousins. The mothers were cradling their sons' bodies wiping the blood from their faces hoping that someone was still alive. When the sisters saw their brothers they cried and slapped their faces in grief covering their faces with their brothers' own blood.

As they began to collect their loved ones, the relatives and elders decided to take the dead bodies to the road leading to Jalalabad and block it in protest, but it wasn't long before a top Russian official found out what was going on. Our tribal leader went to the governor of Jalalabad and told him to come and inspect the bodies and see that there were no Mujahideen among the dead. Why were they killing innocent people?

The governor asked the leader to remove the bodies and said he would come to our village and have a look for himself because the Russian troops claimed to have killed three top Mujahideen commanders. They carried the bodies back to the village graveyard but our imam said these men were martyrs and would go to paradise; they should not suffer anymore so they ought to be buried without further delay because no one believed the Russians would ever come to view the bodies.

As the graves were being covered over, the reality of what had happened slowly began to dawn on me and I started shaking fearing that the tanks would come back, and I wanted to run away. I was also in pain from my broken arm which my mother had tried to set with a stick, some beaten eggs all wrapped in a cloth and held up in a makeshift sling. But our tribal leader told us all to stay. He said they had already killed some of us, so let them return and kill us all.

Suddenly we saw the tanks returning and with them the governor of Jalalabad, Basharmal, together with a senior Russian officer, and they surrounded the area to make sure they themselves would not be attacked. When they were satisfied that there were no weapons, Basharmal again said there were claims that they had killed three Mujahideen commanders who fired the rockets and they insisted that the bodies should be dug up so they could look at the faces. I still remember the Russian officer who came with them. He had many stripes on his uniform, his hat had stars and he had a red face and was very tall. When he saw the bodies he just shook his head and said something in Russian which must have meant they were all innocent people. He removed his hat and bowed three times and walked back to the tanks; Basharmal apologised and promised to do something to help the villagers. He vowed it would not happen again and begged us not to abandon our village. He said we would have his support and he would try to find jobs for the children.

He then began what amounted to a lecture for several minutes saying the Russians were there to help Afghans while the Mujahideen were trying to destroy the country listening only to America and Pakistan. He told us to try and convince our young men not to support the Mujahideen.

That simply angered our tribal leader who asked if that was all he had to say; what about an investigation into the shootings. He said the fact that we had been made to dig up the bodies was even more shameful. He told Basharmal to get out of the village and never return.

The governor said all he could do was regret what had happened and that the Russian officer would conduct an investigation and would arrest those people who did the shooting. Of course, we never heard another thing.

Some people stayed by the graves until evening and the rest of us returned to our homes. I remember no one in the village ate that night despite the fact that there was bread and korma prepared in the mosque for everyone. Nobody touched the food.

That night and much of the next day people were trying to decide what they should do. Some wanted to take revenge and said they should wait until the Mujahideen returned and then they would join them in the fight against the Russians. They had even killed my mother's cousin, Babajan, who had been in the Afghan army. The Russians didn't care who they killed so what was the point of joining the army. They felt it was better to try and free our country and if they got killed they would die as martyrs.

It was not because they wanted to do *jihad* but because they knew who was responsible for ordering the attack and had even led the assault on our village. His name was General Sayed Agha, whose nickname was "*Resh*" meaning beard which made him easily recognisable, and he had done the same thing in other villages. They say Dr Mohammad Najibullah, then president of Afghanistan, loved him because he was a killing machine.

Much later when the Mujahideen took control of the capital, Kabul, the general fled to Pakistan because he didn't have a chance to escape to Russia. One of the top commanders of Gulbuddin Hekmatyar, leader of the Hezb-e Islami party, spoke to some of our villagers who by then were living in Pakistan and said he knew where the general was hiding but he wanted them to witness his arrest as they intended to shoot him in front of everyone in Peshawar. But those poor people said their children were martyrs and some years had passed so they did not want to get involved in this matter again. They were worried that his relatives might find out that they were there and come after them. In the end he was caught and shot in the head and his picture was in the newspaper as the man who had killed so many innocent people in Jalalabad and different provinces.

While a few wanted to fight on, very many of the villagers felt there was no future as there were bound to be more attacks and they would die. There was no protection from the Mujahideen, who were actually putting their lives in danger, and the Russians didn't seem to care about innocent people. So the following night my family, my father and two uncles and another near relative decided to leave the village, go to Pakistan and live as refugees. My two uncles said they would get their families safely to Pakistan but were still determined to return to join the Mujahideen, but my father said if the Mujahideen had not come to our village and fired their rockets in the first place then the 15 men would still be alive. It was not our fight. He said his own father had fought the British when they were in Afghanistan but what had been achieved? We were still poor and we were still suffering so there was no point continuing to struggle. Anywhere, he must have thought, was better than what we already had in our village.

My uncles agreed hoping that at the very least they would find a job in Pakistan and be able to feed their families. They believed, as we all did, that in the end they would be safer in another country.

My mother, however, was not happy and she was frightened that we might be killed on the way, but women had no right to argue so she could not go against her husband's wishes. The decision had been taken. We would be leaving our homes and walking away from the farm we had built up; it must have been terrible for my parents.

As for me, I was excited about leaving and the prospects of going to a new country as only a boy could be. Pakistan sounded modern, even thrilling, in other words everything that Kushgumbad could not offer. I was six and I dreamt they would give us a new house with electricity and we would not have to live in darkness with no running water. Every day I had to help my mom carry buckets of water back to our house, stopping to rest on the way. I was too young and all I could think was that I would at last be safe in Pakistan. I remember we were the first family to leave after that attack but gradually others followed abandoning everything, even our animals, perhaps dreaming that one day we would all return.

One of the Mujahideen had always said he wanted to buy our horses but my father hated him and refused. He never liked them, even when they said they were fighting for the country and, when we eventually went to Pakistan, he kept calling them troublemakers even though I warned him not to be caught saying such things as people would believe he was a communist, but he didn't stop. He blamed them for what had happened forcing him to walk away from everything he had known: his home, his farm, even the animals which we just gave away.

My father was right about leaving because our village was soon to be swallowed up in the fighting and virtually all of it was destroyed in Russian attacks. When we left we had hidden all our valuables in our secret hiding place because we couldn't take them with us. Some years later my father decided to go back to our village as it was safer because the Russians were slowly pulling out of the cities, and he thought he might be able to retrieve those belongings, some of which were quite valuable, and bring them back to Pakistan to sell. But when he got there he could barely recognise our home and could not even find the hiding place because there had been so much direct bombing.

Pakistan was the obvious place to go as it was closer and we assumed we would be safe there; I think my father would have preferred to go to Tajikistan but it was too far to walk and in any case we had heard that Pakistan had opened its borders to all refugees and it sounded good.

I imagine as I fell asleep that last night I was planning in my childish way all the exciting adventures which surely lay ahead; perhaps I would have a chance of going to school, make new friends but I certainly didn't even think of the word refugee or what it might mean. My parents would have been sitting round an oil lamp probably deciding what few belongings they would be able to bring with them and worse what precious items they would have to leave behind forever. They would have had no illusions about what lay ahead; they may have hoped for a safer life, but first we had to get to Pakistan. It would be the start of my 11 years as a refugee.

THREE

Flight from Kushgumbad

Before the attack on our village I had heard my parents and uncles talking about Pakistan and what they would do if indeed the Russians did attack us one day. My father had long decided that Pakistan was the only safe option. My mom on the other hand had wondered if it would not be better for us to move somewhere else in Afghanistan which was still peaceful, but my father said if we were not safe next to the airport how were we ever going to be safe anywhere else even in another city because every day the fighting was spreading. His word, of course, was final.

So two days after the attack my father said we would be leaving. As far as I was concerned it must have seemed like good news. At least I was not going to hear the sound of bombs falling anymore, I could wear nice clothes and shoes and the whole world was helping refugees so there would be no more fighting. It would be a peaceful life and by going to school I would become an educated person.

But what do you do when you decide to walk out of your home for the last time? How do you prepare? What do you take? When my father said we would be leaving that night my mom immediately started cooking and gathering together some leftovers from meals the previous day and about 15 onions. She lit a fire in the clay oven and decided to cook 10 chapatti breads, thinking that would be enough for the journey, and if not she thought God is great and some villagers we were sure to pass on the way might give us some bread. My father told us not to worry because there were some green plants growing in the rivers which we could eat and we would survive. I don't remember if we ever had to resort to eating what I suppose was something like seaweed, but equally I was used to being hungry and I never doubted that my parents would find something for us to eat.

My mom had some cash which she planned to change into Pakistani rupees when we reached Peshawar. We couldn't bring much with us and my mom in particular must have looked around our house, probably in tears, at what she would have to abandon. I remember her folding up some light blankets to sleep on and for some reason I left behind my precious catapult which I had become quite skilful at using hunting birds. That may sound unkind in a modern, civilised world but when you have next to nothing to eat anything that makes a meal is allowed. It must have been clear to everyone that this was not to be any sort of hunting trip. Nevertheless, I would have remained happy, even excited about what would have seemed like an adventure to a young boy.

By then one of our cows had died and the other was very thin so we left it to some villagers. I never asked what my father did with his horses but again I am sure he gave them away to a neighbour; he had no other choice.

My father had already taken our few precious belongings – china plates, metal boxes and some little statues – to bury in our hideout which he covered with mats and dirt so people would not give it a second glance but, of course, it was to be no protection when the Soviet bombs were later dropped on our village.

Then as night fell on that last day my father and two uncles left the village and told us to wait until they came back. It was dark as we had no fire burning and we were all a bit scared as the reality of what we were doing began to sink in. Nobody said very much and my mom cried a lot; everything she and my father had built up together was now lost.

When my father and uncles returned we saw they had four or five donkeys with them which they had hired. The owner of the donkeys was to be our guide because we didn't know the way and most importantly we couldn't be sure which villages or Mujahideen groups we could trust. We must have said goodbye to our friends and, no doubt, promised we would return when we could without really believing it. As far as anyone could tell the Russians had too much military might without being able to overcome the Mujahideen who would continue their hit and run attacks in the rural countryside where they had their main stronghold. Far more likely, more and more families would give up the unequal struggle and follow us out of the village. The flight from Afghanistan has been put at hundreds of thousands to millions of refugees during the Soviet invasion.

The first obstacle we faced was crossing the Kabul River which would have been about waist deep for an adult. When we reached the river bank the men began inflating a dried cow skin as a makeshift raft. The four legs were tied and they literally had to blow it up until the skin was full. It was large enough for my mom, another woman and me to sit in the middle while my father and an uncle pushed us across. The raft was then deflated and loaded back onto the donkeys and we set off on our trek. Jalalabad is 128 kilometres from Peshawar by main road and would take just under three hours by car today, but we were walking through the night and we could not simply march along the main road. What lay ahead for our group of 10, including my parents, uncles and aunts, was a 15-night trek along tracks, up steep mountain paths and through undergrowth.

Having crossed the river, my mom climbed on one of the donkeys, held me in front of her and we set off through the bushes which we all called the jungle. Fortunately the weather was good and warm enough even at night that I just wore my *kurta* shirt while being held in my mom's arms. She kept looking back towards our village straining for one last glimpse of our home in the dark. I also looked back a few times but I was only trying to see if we were being followed by Russian tanks as we had been told not to abandon the village. I don't know what they would have done if they had caught us – maybe they would have sent us back or taken any young men to join the army. We had all just been praying that we would be able to cross the river before anyone noticed we had gone because the tanks would not have been able to cross and chase us.

The first six or seven hours of walking was all through bushes, then we reached the foothills of the Hindu Kush mountains where there were places to hide among the rocks. We were told to keep our mouths shut to hide our white teeth and even clench our fists to avoid showing our fingernails which might have been seen by passing helicopters. We could hear them flying overhead – not one but three, four or five. It was constant every day and if we had been seen they would have attacked because the Soviets would have mistaken us for a Mujahideen patrol.

We would walk each night until dawn broke then stopped for a rest while our guide would lead the donkeys well away from our hiding place so any aircraft flying over would think they were just a normal herd of donkeys grazing. When it was time to set off again he would return; this was the routine every day: walk, hide, eat, sleep and walk on again.

I didn't know exactly where we were going in Pakistan just that it would be somewhere safe. It was only when we were resting on our journey and my father was talking about what we would do when we reached Pakistan and they kept mentioning "Pakistan" that I began to understand that this was to be our final destination and presumably we would never be going home to Kushgumbad again. Also I had no idea how long it would take to get there but I was excited by what I thought life would be like.

Just as when we were in our village, there was a constant threat not only from the Russians but also from the Mujahideen patrols that kept stopping us every step of the way. They were well armed, of course, and searched through our belongings checking that we had no weapons but also to see if we had any food they could take. Life for these fighters was not only dangerous but tough. They were not farmers, they could not be seen to be growing crops and everything they ate they would have taken or possibly bought off someone else. Anything we had my mom would hide saying she only had enough food for the children; inevitably our own supplies began to run low but somehow my father kept finding food for us and we ate twice a day.

The Mujahideen fighters kept asking my father and uncles if they had joined the Afghan army or fought with them in the past. They said no that they were just village farmers and the Russians had killed our men so they were not part of any government forces and not even part of the Muja-hideen. All that our little group wanted to do was flee the country and be safe. My uncle had already warned the rest of us to be careful not to take sides with one particular Mujahideen group or another whenever we met them. They all looked the same with their long beards and if we had said we were going to join the Mujahideen they might have shot us on the spot if we had mentioned the wrong group.

It was also the first time my mom wore a burqa in her life. One of the Mujahideen told her that she should behave like a Muslim woman and wear a hijab or burqa because all she was wearing was a scarf, so my mom immediately agreed. This is what is so tragic about what has become of Afghanistan and other parts of the Middle East today. No one could have been more religious and devout than my mom. She had taught me the Koran and how to pray, she prayed constantly herself, even while sitting beside me as we rested on our journey, and yet she was being accused of not being a proper Muslim because she was not covered in a burqa. Is that all it takes to prove you are a good Muslim? They also criticised my father because he was clean shaven apart from a smart moustache. He felt obliged to grow a beard which made him look older, but it never changed his point of view.

On about the third day when we were hiding in the mountains we suddenly heard a loud explosion nearby. We thought that we had been caught by the Russians and now we were about to be lined up and shot. I was shaking and my mind instantly jumped back to the shooting in our village. I prayed and was scared that they would kill all my family and leave me alive. What was I supposed to do here in the middle of nowhere? Who was going to bury all the bodies?

My uncle told us all to keep quiet while he went to see what had happened. He thought a plane must have dropped a bomb it had been so loud.

Eventually he returned carrying a young boy who had lost one leg and his other was hanging by a thread. He can't have been more than six years old. His mother was in shock and couldn't speak then she fainted. My mom sprinkled some water on her face to help her recover and her husband was praying out loud that his son would survive. The boy was losing a lot of blood and I could not understand why he was not crying, but then I realised he was in shock.

The poor boy had trodden on a mine which the Russians had put throughout the countryside to kill the Mujahideen. Our guide warned us all not to wander from the path which had been marked out with stones covered in red paint.

My uncle asked the guide to put the boy on one of his donkeys and take him to the nearest Mujahideen position because they would have had a doctor who looked after their own wounded fighters, and he could treat him. In the evening the guide and the boy's father returned. My father asked how the boy was but there was no reply. I don't think he survived. My mom made me promise never to walk away from the path which I used to do to collect small round stones to play with. It was the worst day of our trek to Pakistan.

As we walked on the men were getting tired and inevitably tempers frayed and the anger grew about what had happened to our village. By the seventh or eighth day I heard my uncles saying that they had had enough. They were going to get guns and join the fighting; maybe the Mujahideen would pay some money if they joined them and they could take revenge for what the Russians had done. But my father kept warning them that if they did that they would not live for long.

For a while I thought of this as an adventure and whenever I saw a river I would say to my father we should stop and catch fish as we used to do in Kushgumbad, and instead of just eating bread and raw onions we could eat some fish. He shouted at me saying we were in a dangerous situation and yet all I could do was think about fishing. He told me to forget all about those days. They were just a dream and we were going to start a new life. He said I should always think about the future and not listen to my uncles talking about joining the Mujahideen because I was too young and didn't understand. He told me firmly just to do what he said and even if he was not around I should not listen to my uncles.

Far from it being a dream, all I could think of as I lay down on my thin blanket, my mother praying by my side, was the nightmare of the cold-blooded shooting of the 15 men at home and their blood being carried away by the river. It was a recurring horror that I remembered in my sleep for months afterwards.

The walk was slow and hard going. I was lucky because I was with my mom on a donkey but my father's feet were covered in blisters. Every time we stopped to rest and he took off his *chappals* – open sandals – my mom would rub his feet with some sort of soothing ointment she had. We walked in single file in the mountainside which was controlled by

Mujahideen and occasionally we heard the sound of Kalashnikovs being fired in the distance but we were never caught up in a fight.

Another day we saw a convoy of maybe 35 Russian tanks which took at least half an hour to pass by. Although we were some distance away and well hidden it was a frightening moment. They weren't looking for us but if we had been seen they would surely have called in a gunship to attack. From what we could tell they seemed to be heading towards the Pakistan border and my mom thought there was going to be a war between Pakistan and the Soviet Union which we were walking straight into. She said we should turn back because Pakistan was going to be even more dangerous than taking our chances in Kushgumbad, but my father said we should continue.

We passed through some villages but they had no food to spare. In one place we tried to pay for a ride on a truck but it was full and there was no space for such a large group, so we went on walking following tracks familiar to the guide who earned his living helping refugees trying to escape the fighting.

Some of the mountain paths were even difficult for the donkeys so my mom and I would get off and the men would have to pull them or push from behind. There was nothing I could do as a child and, in any case, my arm was still in a sling. It was itchy from the egg solution my mom had used to speed up the healing process but not as painful as it had been. In fact, I was beginning to get bored and I would throw my stones into the rivers we passed. This just made my father shout at me to stop making a noise; I had no idea of the potential danger we were all in.

If I was not throwing stones I would fall asleep against my mom and so would she, resulting in us both nearly tumbling off the donkey. It made my father angry and he would prod her with his stick to keep her awake saying she should sleep during the day and not risk allowing me to fall. But it was hard for everyone; hard to sleep during the day, hard for the men to walk through the night, hard for my mom to keep hold of me.

As we got closer to the border we no longer had to hide from Soviet gunships as the area was completely under the control of the Mujahideen, so we could walk during the day which made the going easier. The mood seemed to improve as new people kept joining us forming a long line and by the time we were getting near the border more people just seemed to appear especially the women because it was safer for them to be in a group. Some women were alone bringing with them young children aged just four or five, but no men at all. My father let the women and children join us as they were in the same state: frightened, hungry and just desperate to find any sanctuary, but he would have refused if there had been any men among them because he could not be sure who they supported. Trust among strangers, even fellow Afghans, had been lost, probably forever. We had started out as a group of 10 but by the time we reached the border after 13 nights we were 70 or 80 and the bigger the number the more our confidence grew; there was safety in numbers or so it seemed.

When we stopped to rest on the way the women would sit together and share their experiences. Each woman we met had lost a family member in the fighting; some had lost their husbands, others their brothers. My mother told them that she had lost her cousins and there would be a lot of crying. She urged some of the younger ones to find another husband and try to start a new life, but they would say no, they had already got children and they would now concentrate on bringing them up, but what really lay ahead no one knew.

We didn't even know when we crossed the border into Pakistan because there were no signs or control points, but on the 13th or 14th day our guide left us taking his donkeys with him. I remember that day clearly as I had to start walking myself. The other noticeable thing was we started seeing small shops. That year maybe three or four million refugees had fled into Pakistan from different directions so it was quite enterprising of the shopkeepers as they realised that all the refugees would need supplies with their food and water running low. Someone can always make a profit out of another person's misfortune, but I don't blame them as they also needed to live.

When we had crossed the border we saw that everybody seemed to be openly carrying guns. My father explained that they were tribal people who were allowed to have guns so I shouldn't be scared but I should avoid staring at them which was hard for me as everything I saw was new and exciting.

The first thing my father did was to try and get us a ride on one of the many lorries crammed with people to reach a refugee camp – in fact my father didn't know which camp we would be going to; he didn't even know if there was more than one. He paid a driver who said he would take us as far as Karkhano, a district in Peshawar, but he could not go any further into the city. We clambered aboard. There were no seats, of course, with everyone standing in the back of the lorry – there may have been about 25 of us.

We didn't have any money for accommodation so when we reached Karkhano we kept asking how we could get to the Afghan refugee camp, which we had heard about. We found another bigger lorry which could take 200 people with men climbing on top and others clinging to the sides. It cost 400 rupees for the family. My mom and I and another woman sat in the front with the driver, I was on my mom's lap so as not to take up space while my father hung on to the side of the lorry.

Finally we reached Shamshatu camp which lies 25 kilometres south-east of Peshawar City. As far as I knew this was to be my future and I can only think that I must have wondered where my home was that I had been dreaming about, the electricity and running water. Where was I going to find my new friends? Where was I going to go to school?

Today when I look back I wonder how we ever managed to make the journey – I certainly wouldn't be able to do it again.

FOUR

Arrival in refugee camp

As we clambered down from the lorry clutching our few precious belongings my parents must have looked with horror at what was before them. Shamshatu – it means tortoise in Pashto – was once a barren stretch of land handed over to Gulbuddin Hekmatyar in 1982 by General Zia for him to establish a refugee camp, but it was also used as a training facility for his faction of the Mujahideen – Zia's most favoured group of the "Peshawar Seven".

The reality was the camp was funded by Zia with support from America and Saudi Arabia. I saw a lot of Arab Mujahideen commanders coming to the camp to visit Hekmatyar offering their backing and I presume financial support without which the camp could not have prospered as it did. It is said that of all the weaponry and money Zia received, 50% would go to Hekmatyar and the rest divided among the other six factions.

I asked one of my uncles what the Arabs were doing in the camp and he told me they were our guests and helping us to do *jihad* in Afghanistan because we had lost more than a million people and now the Arabs were here to join us. But my father gave a totally different explanation telling me: "Son, don't even go near them. They are here to destroy our country and they will create big problems in the region."

My father always blamed President Reagan for creating the Mujahideen and President George Bush Senior for sending Arabs from their countries to join the fight. But the Arabs were different –

they looked different and they sounded different. They had good, clean clothes, jumpers, boots, guns, money and cars and clearly enjoyed a better lifestyle than the Mujahideen and certainly better than the thousands of refugees like us. They attended our local mosques for daily prayers but the teaching was all about the benefits of *jihad* in Islam even though they were praying differently from the rest of us because they were the more extreme and ultra-conservative Muslim Wahabis from Saudi Arabia and we were all Sunni Muslims. All they succeeded in doing was dividing the camp – some people began to hate them while others started following them and their Wahabi ideas. Nothing was left to chance as they pushed their message keeping Pashto and Farsi interpreters with them at all times.

By the time our family arrived at the camp in 1985 it was well-established with probably 10,000 refugees – over the years it would grow to more than 50,000 providing a steady supply of future fighters for Hekmatyar. But far from there being a new home for us with electricity and running water it was a sea of tents stretching before our eyes, the odd mud brick house in those early days and in the centre a big mosque. My parents and I were allocated one tent which was to be our new home where we lived, cooked and slept. This wasn't the dream I had been thinking about on our walk. This was worse than our home and infinitely worse than even our simple life in Afghanistan. I can only guess that on that first day when we sat down in the tent, exhausted after our walk from Kushgumbad, my parents must have stared at each other in bewilderment, my father wondering what he had done to his family. This was not what was promised or at least talked about when they were planning their new life in Pakistan; I would have just sat there waiting to be told what was supposed to happen next, certain that this was not to be our new home forever. After all, where would we keep animals, where would I go to school, where were my friends?

What would happen next became all too clear on the second day. My mom gave me a large plastic bag and told me to go out in search of wood or plastic to make a fire and not to return until the bag was full. She also told me to pick up any plastic bottles or tin cans which could be sold according to their weight. Needless to say every other child in the camp was doing exactly the same thing which meant walking further and further in search of scraps to collect; most days I would be gone for four hours before returning to our tent, my shoulders aching from the load. It was very hot and the dust would be thrown up by the Mujahideen racing through the camp on their motorbikes or in 4x4s, all heavily armed with guns and anti-tank rocket launchers; every week we saw boxes of bullets and guns arriving regularly in convoys of 10 or 15 cars. Whereas in our home village we might have seen a few Mujahideen from time to time, we were clearly living in the heart of a Mujahideen training camp; this was Hekmatyar's base and headquarters. They were in control and imposed the rules in the camp. The Pakistani police were not even allowed in although they had check points outside the perimeter.

One section of the camp was strictly off limits to everyone except the fighters. This was where Hekmatyar's men were being trained under the direction of Pakistan's ISI (Inter Services Intelligence). There was no live firing but the men came out covered in sweat carrying their Kalashnikovs so it was obviously very tough physical training. I actually saw General Hamid Gul, then ISI's Director General, twice at the camp hugging Hekmatyar in greeting. They were like brothers. Gul spoke in the mosque in Urdu translated into Pashto. It was no prayer meeting, rather a motivational speech talking about bringing Islam to the world and how Afghans would control the whole of India one day and soon the whole of the Western world. In fact none of the regular calls to prayer had anything to do with the Koran. Every day Hekmatyar spoke about driving the Russians out of Afghanistan and doing *jihad*, which was tempting for many because they were being offered $800 to become fighters. You either survived on handouts or you joined the other fighters taking the money on offer; it must have sounded appealing to young men with nothing else to do but sit in their tents.

My father didn't join Hekmatyar's faction but when I turned seven they insisted that I should start going to the mosque every day and attending the madrassa religious school where there was a class of maybe 60 or 70 children and lessons lasted for two or three hours. They taught us the Koran and gave us a book of prayers after which I went off to collect firewood.

There were no parties and no music, of course. After all, there seemed little to celebrate for the refugees; I don't even recall much laughter. When a couple got married it was another seemingly unhappy gathering when the bridegroom attended the mosque with his male friends, the imam said a few prayers and then they all went to the bride's "home" where she was asked three times if she accepted the man as her husband as is the tradition and if she said yes, they were married. Where was the joy in that, where was the celebration?

There can be no doubt that my father regretted leaving our village the moment he laid eyes on the refugee camp; most of the time my mom was crying and asking how we were going to survive. My father tried to reassure her saying one day the Russians would pull out and we would rebuild our home in Kushgumbad but it was another promise he probably knew that he could not keep. The Russians seemed too strong at that stage and no matter how bravely the Mujahideen fought they were not making an impact.

As the weeks passed by my father became very sad. I now realise that he was suffering some sort of depression. He had left his home assuming that he would at least be under Pakistani control, but instead we found ourselves under the harsh regime of Hekmatyar. There were restrictions at every turn: shaving was banned, something many people think was introduced by the Taliban, but it was brought in by Hekmatyar before them. Women were never allowed out of their tents alone and if they wanted to go to the little shops they had to be accompanied by a male, even if it was a boy like me. My mom was used to total freedom at home where she had the responsibility of our animals, milking the cows, but now she was a virtual prisoner in her tent not even allowed fresh air, such as it was in the camp.

We could hear a lot of noise from other children in the tents nearby but we rarely saw them because the women seldom came out. I managed to make a few friends but we had to go outside the camp to play whenever we were not praying in the mosque, attending the madrassa or collecting firewood. Such was the daily routine and I must have longed for those walks to my aunt carrying milk to her or even helping my father in the fields or better still going fishing. I never forget the day when my father slapped me in my face when he found me playing marbles with some other children. I know he was just overreacting because of the pressure he was under but he didn't even want me to play marbles because he thought that I would learn about gambling, even though it was only winning or losing marbles.

Every week the Arab Red Crescent would come and put up more tents as the refugees streamed in day after day. Survival, as usual, was at the forefront of our minds. From one day to the next we could not be sure where the next meal was coming from and it would have been the same for the thousands of other refugees, most of whom had next to no money. There was a monthly ration card system to get bread, some oil and other food but there was no clean running water so every day we had to stand in a long queue at a hand pump to fill our containers. I don't think I showered for more than a month.

Those who could afford it travelled into Peshawar city to buy extra food or clothes for themselves or to stock up the shops selling groceries in the camp. We never did because we didn't have enough money. In fact my father never even gave me two rupees to buy a ball to play with. On rare occasions he bought some meat or received handouts from the Red Crescent whenever they visited to give vaccinations to the children.

There were no restrictions on coming or going at the camp; indeed, every day we could see long lines of new refugees arriving so it would have been difficult to control the flow even if they had wanted to stop new people arriving. As far as I recall there was little crime actually in the camp where Hekmatyar's people were very strict although gangs would go into Peshawar city to see what they could steal. Later I read that as the numbers grew a prison was established and punishment was severe, even torture according to some reports.

All along my father tried to persuade his brothers not to join Hekmatyar's people but I think he must have lost any influence over them; after all he had been promising a new life and a new beginning in Pakistan and it had not been true. His brothers felt they had no option but to do *jihad* so they joined Hezb-e Islami and before long were fighting regularly; the younger one, Ghulam Haidar, of course, became a top commander. Every so often he would leave the camp and his wife for two or three months at a time to fight in Afghanistan against the Russians before returning. Many of his followers would have come from Shamshatu but others would have been based in Afghanistan.

There were clearly rows among the brothers and one of them said to my father if he didn't want to do *jihad* at least keep quiet so the family didn't have any trouble in the camp with Hekmatyar. I am sure they blamed him for persuading them to leave their village in the first place, but my father's view was even if he died in the process he was not happy in the camp. The Russians may not have killed us but the stress of living in the camp and seeing people with guns and rocket launchers every day was making him ill and it would kill him as surely as the Russians.

After some six months in Shamshatu my father decided he could take it no longer. Every day he and his brothers had long arguments about what they had done and what was the right thing to do now. My father knew leaving Shamshatu would be a hard decision because he feared his brothers would become even more extreme *jihadis* and also he didn't want to move somewhere else where we would be alone without any relatives, but he must have felt he had no choice.

When we first arrived in Pakistan we just asked for "the refugee camp" without knowing if there were any others and we were taken to Shamshatu. But my father found out that there was another camp in a district called Kababyan run by Sayyid Ahmed Gailani. He had created a party called the National Islamic Front of Afghanistan after fleeing to Pakistan himself. His party was another of the Peshawar Seven but was more liberal rejecting both communism and Islamism. Clearly my father decided that this sounded a better place to be, assuming we had to remain as refugees somewhere. The difficulty was leaving Shamshatu.

I clearly remember the evening when my father came back to the tent looking very tired and sad. I looked at him and tried to hug him but he pushed me away and told me to go and get my uncles and tell them to meet him.

I walked to their tents and found one uncle and told him my father wanted to see him right away. He asked what had happened and wondered if my father had hit my mom again. I say again because the week before I ran crying to my uncle saying my father had hit my mom with a pot full of green tea and cut her forehead. I am sorry to say that in a society like Afghanistan where men always have the last word, it is normal for them to sometimes mistreat women. On that occasion my father was getting angry and shouting for no reason at all, although

I know now that he was so depressed and regretted ever having left Kushgumbad.

I told him no, my father just needed to talk to him. My father said to him that he had made his mind up to move from Shamshatu and go to Gailani's camp near Peshawar because he could find work in the city and be safe there.

My uncle said the only way to leave without raising suspicions with Hekmatyar was to say he had found a relative living in Peshawar who had agreed to take him and the family in. This explanation was accepted and, having failed one last time to convince his uncles to join us, we collected our possessions, such as they were, left our tent early the next morning and took another lorry ride to Peshawar.

FIVE

Russian defeat – a new dawn

When we arrived at Gailani's camp we saw what looked like millions of refugees – whatever the precise number it was much bigger than Shamshatu. The majority were Pashtuns and were supporters of Hekmatyar but there was a definite difference. The atmosphere seemed less tense and there were fewer guns on display and overall less pressure. Gailani himself was a moderate man and even wore a short beard, while his commanders, who seemed more educated, ran the refugee camp in an area called Kabadyan. We were given a new Gailani refugee ID card and provided with a tent as he was getting a lot of support and funds from UNHCR and other organisations helping Afghan refugees.

Young men did not have to join Gailani's fighters although many did and the mosques were always full with crowds spilling out into the street. The message, however, was still the same: to do *jihad* and drive out the Russian infidel should be every Afghan's moral duty and that duty was made clear to everyone from an early age.

After two weeks my father registered me in one of the refugee schools next to the camp called Sidiq Akbar, which was run by Gailani's people. I was so excited because for the first time in my life I would be able to study proper subjects like Farsi, Pashto, history, maths and the Koran with about 50 other children. The school provided us with free text books, notebooks, pens and pencils; it was one of my happiest moments for a long time and a complete contrast to life in Shamshatu. I enjoyed our lessons, worked hard and from class one to class three I always came top.

However, one day when I was doing my homework and reading aloud in our tent my father asked me to show him my text book. He looked at it and found the words I was learning were "M" for Mujahideen, "J" for *jihad* and "K" for Kalashnikov. He shook his head and said I was in the wrong school and he didn't want me to be brainwashed with that sort of education, but he could not simply go to the teacher and complain. There had to be another solution.

It is depressing to think that nothing has changed in the intervening 30-odd years. I have seen YouTube videos of classes full of seven-year-olds just like me being instructed in exactly the same way learning the meaning of *jihad* and even being shown a Kalashnikov in the classroom and being told it was to be used to kill the infidel. At least there was no actual gun in my class but there were plenty of pictures and even some wooden guns painted to look like Kalashnikovs. I brought one back to our tent one day and my father asked what I was doing with it. I said a friend gave it to me and he just broke it over his knee and said all it was good for was the fire. But I had to continue at the school as there was no alternative.

In fact, there were fewer guns generally on display as ordinary people – not fighters – were not allowed to carry them because it was considered disrespectful to our neighbours. Commanders, of course, were always heavily armed and accompanied by their bodyguards.

Life was much better in the camp for my parents than what they had had to endure in Shamshatu as everything was altogether more relaxed. My mom didn't have to wear a burqa and could sit outside chatting to other women comparing their experiences and my father was able to shave his beard again. When I saw that my mum could move about freely and go to the shops and my father was confident that he could leave her while he went in search of work in Peshawar, I too felt more relaxed and happier. However, I still had to collect firewood every day and look for bottles and cans to sell. Our daily food was also still basic: our breakfast usually consisted of dry bread dipped in tea with sugar and in the afternoon my mom would cook up some tomatoes and onions with water as our main meal. Once a week when my father was making some money he would buy a kilo of meat. We got free milk, which I think came from Saudi Arabia and food from the Red Crescent in Kuwait, although there was still no electricity or running water; every evening water tankers arrived and we filled our containers that way, which was an improvement on the hand pump in Shamshatu.

We also had to collect water in buckets when it rained because our tent was flimsy and full of holes so it leaked during the rainy season even though my father put some plastic sheeting over the top. When I heard the sound of thunder I started shaking and we all prayed to Allah to stop the rain. Some people like the sound of raindrops but I hate it because it reminds me of those terrible times. The tent, which we lived in for about three years, was only just big enough for the three of us and there was no room for a proper bed so we just put pillows and blankets down on the bare ground. We built a small shelter outside which was big enough for one person to sit in to cook and make tea; in fact the living conditions were much worse in this camp than Shamshatu, although not for Gailani himself. He was among the richest of all the leaders and lived in a big, luxurious house surrounded by heavily armed guards about four kilometres from the camp which we saw in the distance every time we went to school. He never visited our camp and most of his followers from Kandahar were in tents outside the camp.

Our tent was so torn and shredded that my mom told my father to go and see Gailani himself to get a letter from him to authorise a replacement. But my father said he didn't want to be like one refugee family who went to see Maulana Yunis Khalis, who had led a group also called Hezb-e Islami. When they asked for his help he just took off his jacket and threw it at them saying he didn't have anything to give them and they should just take the jacket off his back. Khalis's action was so famous it had made the papers which was why my mom told my father to go to Gailani.

Father refused so my mom told me to let her know when any outsiders were visiting the camp. When I saw one group arriving – they were Pakistanis and English – I told my mom and she shouted at them to come and look at the state of our tents. When they saw how bad ours was, as well as the tents next to us, they wrote everything down and took pictures, and they ordered new tents which we were given the very next day. They came quickly because there was a big storage depot just outside the camp where they had everything: oil, rice, flour and tents which were distributed when we showed our ration cards. I have no idea who those people were but they must have had some influence to get such a quick reaction.

We used to get quite a few international visitors at this camp and I think that must have been because Gailani was better connected – he wanted King Zahir Shah to return from exile in Italy and run the country because he was not an outsider and my father felt that only he truly understood the Afghan mentality.

On one occasion a large number of Pakistani soldiers suddenly arrived and spread out through the camp asking the Mujahideen not to show their weapons. They were followed by another group of army vehicles and out stepped Princess Diana who was met by the leader of the camp and presented with an Afghan rug. It was a very short visit, maybe 10 or 15 minutes, but she came to talk mainly to amputees and offer them some comfort. She had a large box of sweets which she threw out to the children gathering around her, but I was too far away to catch one, and then, just as suddenly, she was gone.

We saw a lot of American, German and French visitors from various charities who came to see the camp for themselves and to take photos. We were all lined up and stared at the cameras hoping that they would put their hands in their pockets and give us some money, but it never happened; they just wanted their pictures for magazines and newspapers in the West. The most famous and iconic refugee photo was of Sharbat Gula taken by Steve McCurry in 1984 and it appeared on the front cover of the National Geographic magazine. The award-winning image of Sharbat's green eyes staring straight at the camera helped raise the profile of the Afghan war for a time in international media.

Another visitor in 1987 was Osama bin Laden who was still not that well known. It was the first time I saw him and he arrived in a convoy of 4x4s. He sat next to the driver with six bodyguards behind him armed with guns and rocket launchers.

I believe Abu Musab al-Zarqawi, the Jordanian *jihadist*, was in the second car. He was a young man in his 20s then and not famous at all but later became notorious for bombings and beheadings in the 2003

Iraq war. They had all come to meet Dr Iman al-Zawahiri. The men and children ran after them chanting Allahu Akbar as they were so well regarded among the people because they were doing *jihad* in Afghanistan. They announced on a loudspeaker that if there were any Arabs in the camp they needed to come together. I believe bin Laden was trying to unite all the Arabs into one group because he had a plan to create what would become known as al-Qaeda the following year. Al-Zawahiri would later succeed bin Laden as leader of al-Qaeda.

There were no restrictions on visitors from other camps and my uncle, Ghulam Haidar, the Mujahideen commander, would come from time to time. He clearly had regrets about the fighting he was involved in and my father told him he should have listened to him when he said that we were all Muslims and we respected *jihad* but this was not true *jihad*. He told him that the fighting had not only set Afghans against the Russians, but Afghans against Afghans – thousands of lives had been lost. But my uncle was both angry and sad. They kept losing men in the fighting and when he saw all the refugees just sitting around the camp he thought they should have joined the other Mujahideen in the struggle. He always had his head covered and bowed; he never smiled and I certainly never saw him laughing.

Every Ramadan, people from Saudi Arabia came in big lorries loaded with dates as a gift but the dates were old, dry and covered in sand so we had to wash them before eating. I think they just wanted to get rid of them. This was the only food we got from Saudi Arabia but, of course, they sent us many men to be trained to fight the Russians in Afghanistan – that was their other "gift" to us.

My parents were always quiet over Ramadan and never celebrated like others because they were remembering the good times they used to enjoy with friends in Kushgumbad. Most of the other kids got new clothes and shoes then but I didn't and I am sure that was why my father didn't like me going out on Eid days because he didn't want me to see the other kids in their new clothes and was ashamed. I don't blame him because my father didn't have the money to spare; instead every day he left the tent searching for jobs in Peshawar. I never asked him what sort of work he was doing but sometimes he looked so tired and would ask my mom to massage his shoulders. Later he told me that he was emptying lorries full of bags of rice and flour weighing about 40 kilos and carrying them to a warehouse.

The biggest celebration every year was when the seven leaders came together for a big gathering to protest against the Soviet occupation with everyone waving flags and guns, and cheering. Hundreds of lorries arrived bringing maybe 50 or 60 thousand people to an area called Hayatabad, which today is a modern suburb of Peshawar but then was open land. We spent all day there listening to speeches calling us to do *jihad*.

One year, 15 of us boys were chosen to recite a *Tirana* in Arabic to all the seven tribal leaders before the ceremony started. It was in Arabic because they wanted to convince more Arabic people to support us. There were many important Arab guests and people from Pakistan invited to these gatherings along with other Islamic leaders. We chanted for maybe five minutes and then we all shook hands with the leaders and everyone was cheering and clapping. I was so proud to meet Hekmatyar without, of course, being fully aware of what he was doing; one year they let him speak first and he talked for an hour, but when he finished everyone started leaving because they had all come to listen to him and they were not interested in what the others had to say. The next year they didn't let Hekmatyar speak first!

The only news we heard from the outside world was from my father's very small transistor radio. I always had to keep quiet when he was listening to BBC Pashto or Farsi with the little radio pressed to his ear. I remember him laughing when reporters would call the Mujahideen "heroes" fighting the Soviets. Why didn't they just call them fighters, he would ask. He never wanted to miss the news because he was waiting to hear if the Russians were leaving so we could go back home. In 1988 news began filtering through of peace agreements being reached between Afghanistan, the USSR, the USA and Pakistan, and of Soviet troops beginning to pulling out. The Russian President Gorbachev was trying to create a new government in Afghanistan so he could withdraw his forces, and my father would keep telling us that the fighting might soon be over.

Finally, in 1989, the Soviet army did pull out their last troops and the refugees in camp were all celebrating and cheering in the streets at the news. We also heard about the collapse of the Berlin Wall that same year so finally we thought there might be peace, although my father said America should stay and press the Afghans to create their own government and run their own country themselves.

Gradually more refugees began heading home but my father was still worried. He heard on the news that the Hezb e-Islami and another group, Jamayat e-Islami, founded by Burhanuddin Rabbani, were now fighting each other, which sparked another row with his brother. Where was *jihad* now, he would ask him; the Russians had gone but Afghans were instead killing one another in their bid for power. Dr Najibullah's government, propped up by the Soviets, was under threat and the country still faced years of civil war.

My mom wanted us to stay in Pakistan because the government was not going to force us to leave. As my father was working and earning money and the camp was emptying they decided that they should find somewhere else to live either in another camp or in accommodation in Peshawar. But they wanted to get away from the camps forever so they began looking for somewhere more permanent which they could call home in Peshawar. My father had also started polishing shoes in the city setting up his shoe shine stand outside a mosque which meant he was now earning a little more, probably 60 rupees a day, and was confident about finding a room large enough for us all.

The other bright news in 1989 was the birth of my brother, Ahmed, while we were still in the refugee camp. As he was born the same year the Russians left Afghanistan my mother called him "the luckiest child", unlike me! I remember early that morning I was kicked out of the tent and an elderly woman came in to help my mom with the birth.

Every day people came to congratulate her and gave her 20 rupees as a gift. In return my father had bought a large sack of peanuts and, as is the tradition, gave the well-wishers a handful to thank them. By contrast when my sister, Wahida, was born some years later no one came. I asked my mom why no one had congratulated her and she said it was because she was a girl. I couldn't understand what she meant as she was still a newborn baby like my brothers, but this is the culture. They don't like girls and I don't think it is likely to change even though the prophet, Muhammad, said this was wrong and that girls were the same as boys. In Afghanistan, as is the case in many Islamic cultures, fathers don't appreciate daughters because they are regarded as a financial burden. There are many examples in my village where men marry two or three girls because the first wives haven't given birth to boys. But the day after Ahmed was born my proud father took him straight to the mosque for the imam to whisper the *adhaan,* the Muslim call to prayer, in his right ear.

One thing my brother did not get, just like me, was a birth certificate because refugee children born in camps and even in hospitals in Pakistan were not allowed Pakistani citizenship – their ID always stated Citizen of Afghanistan. Some people in the camp would say to my father that he should apply for a Pakistani ID card but he refused, saying he was an Afghan.

Many years later when my own first daughter was born in Pakistan I tried to register her birth but because I could not provide my own birth certificate I was turned away. So I went to the bazaar in Peshawar and found a shop where they just printed a copy saying my daughter was born in Afghanistan. Millions of other refugee family babies born in Pakistan still have to say on their birth certificates that they were born in Afghanistan.

Slowly but surely our camp began to empty as refugees moved to different camps where they were being paid $800 to return home or they went directly back to Afghanistan; others decided to stay for good in Pakistan because thousands of children had been born in the camps and their families felt that was where their future lay.

When I saw my classmates beginning to leave I asked my parents what we would be doing. My mom told me that our house in Kush-gumbad had been destroyed and they didn't want to get caught up in the fighting which was now raging between rival Muslim factions. By chance my father had met some Pakistanis in his workplace and they had recommended a landlord with property in Tehkal Payan, which is near Peshawar airport. They agreed a rent of 400 Pakistani rupees a month, the equivalent of about £2 sterling, plus our electricity and water bills, which we had to take to the landlord's house in cash.

I was thrilled to be told that we would be living in a proper house with electricity and running water for the first time in my life aged 10 years. We collected everything we possessed and, with the help of some other refugees to carry our boxes, we walked out of the camp and half an hour later reached our new home.

SIX

Shoe shine boy

It may seem like a small comfort but for the first time in my life I was living in a house with concrete walls not mud bricks or worse still leaking canvas sides. It still was a house with a wooden roof but above all it had electricity and running water. I had never experienced such things before – I was living in luxury. We didn't have the whole house to ourselves, of course; we just rented one of the four rooms, but it was dry, secure and safe. At last, I thought, I could start living a new and better life. It was 1990 and I was 11.

The good news was we were able to gather our relatives around us because first one uncle arrived with his wife and took a room, then the second uncle took another room with his family and a cousin took the fourth room. I can only assume that word got back to other relatives because before long more arrived setting up their tents in the large courtyard until we soon had 15 families all living together.

The landlord, who had a good heart, said we had set up our own mini refugee camp but allowed us all to stay just raising the rent eventually to 1,800 rupees to cover the extra families. We all shared the power supply which inevitably meant there were regular power cuts and we had to get an electrician in to fix the problem. It wasn't surprising as one way we had of boiling the water for our tea was to stick a cable into the pot.

There were no kitchens so those of us who had rooms lived, slept and cooked in the same room which soon proved dangerous. To build a fire we would collect hot coals from a nearby kiln where they made bricks and brought them back in buckets which my mom would use to heat our meals in a corner of the room. It wasn't long before we all developed coughs and someone told us that we were killing ourselves with all the smoke in the room from the burning coals despite the open window. It seems obvious now but until that point we had been used to living in cramped conditions, so from then on we did all the cooking in the courtyard.

While we may have been safe from the fighting in Afghanistan it was still going on and threatening the capital, Kabul, which created a new group of refugees whom we would describe as being posh and educated. They were different in many ways not least in their appearance. The women didn't wear burqas and the men were clean shaven, which had a remarkable effect on the Pakistani women who soon stopped wearing burqas themselves when they saw the Kabul women walking around freely without face coverings. But unlike the rest of us they didn't go to refugee camps such as Shamshatu; instead they could afford to rent smart houses in Peshawar.

Best of all, as far as I was concerned, was they built a school near our home which I joined. It was directly opposite the Peshawar airport runway where we could see the planes taking off and landing. The head teacher and all the other teachers were female but it was a mixed school for boys and girls called Bibi Zainab, named after the eldest daughter of the prophet Muhammad, and it quickly became one of the most popular schools in our area.

One thing I hoped to be able to stop doing when we moved into our house was collecting extra firewood and tin cans from the street, but it was still necessary. One day I was carrying a bag in the city and some of the students from my school saw me. I tried to hide my face but I couldn't and one of them recognised me calling my name. I didn't want to look at them in case they talked about me picking up litter at school. But they did tell their mother, who was a teacher, that they had seen me carrying bags with scrap paper and cans. When I got to school the next day she called me into her office and told me that she understood my situation because her children had seen me near their home picking through the rubbish. But she said there was nothing to feel embarrassed about and that she had told her own children not to talk to the other pupils about it. She told me to carry on with my studies and that my family should be proud of me for what I was doing to help. Then the teacher started to collect shoes that needed repairing from other members of staff and gave them to me in a bag for my father to polish and repair, paying 500 rupees which was far too much as my father would only charge 2 rupees for each pair. It was a wonderful gesture because she didn't just want to give me money like a beggar out of charity.

One of my cousins was also in the school in the same class as me, and there was always a bit of rivalry between us. He tried to beat me and come top of the class, but he never managed to come higher than 5th or 6th. I think he was a bit jealous of me but there would be greater problems than that for both of us to face.

In the meantime, in1991, my second brother, Nur, was born but, of course, there was no birth certificate and my father got a fake Afghan ID paper from the bazaar which was handwritten with a photo and a forged stamp just like so many others. There were plenty of family and friends around in our little mini-refugee camp to celebrate but there were also problems looming.

Two years later my school received a warning letter from Hekmatyar ordering the head teacher to separate the boys from the girls immediately. The very next day when we went to the school our teachers were crying and gave me and the other boys our papers and told us to ask our fathers to find a school for boys. It was devastating news not just because at last I had settled into a proper school where professional teachers were teaching academic subjects, but because of all the personal support I was getting from the staff.

But when we were told that we had to leave the school the teachers said they would go on sending their shoes to my father for repair; they always gave me 10 or 15 shoes to mend which really was a form of financial support from them; most of the staff were from Kabul and had a good heart and would pay me 200 or 300 rupees. It was an enormous sum of money for us and when I got home I gave it to my father.

We found another school, Omar Sani, which was about 40 minutes' walk from our house. However, all the subjects were taught in Pashto which was not easy for me as it was not my first language and I got beaten regularly by the religious teacher for making mistakes when I was reciting the Koran. I tried to hide the slap marks on my face from my father because I didn't want him to overreact even though it amounted to a form of abuse. One morning while I was still sleeping my father saw the bruises and he woke me up and asked what had happened. I told him that one of the religious teachers, a man called Zaman Khan, was always slapping me because I didn't understand Pashto. He was furious and immediately went to the school. I tried to tell him it was alright and that it was not that bad because I knew that if he complained they would throw me out of the school. But he was really upset and demanded to see the head teacher and immediately started swearing at him about the treatment a so-called religious man was handing out. The religious teacher, who was a Pashtun himself, hid, but all the other teachers came out when they heard the shouting. My father took all the books out of my school bag and tore them up one by one then marched me out of the school. That was the last day of my education. I was 13 years old.

My father told me not to blame him for ending my education. He said these Mujahideen schools were a waste of time anyhow and now it was time for me to acquire a professional skill and earn money, so I started to learn how to polish and repair shoes like him. I still wanted to have a better education and every day I tried to persuade my father to find another school for me but he didn't want to listen. He said he was getting old and he wanted me to learn how to make money to support the family.

After a few months I learned enough to polish and repair shoes on my own while my father left me to go and pray in the mosque to get out of the summer heat. At least, I thought I knew enough. One day a man came and asked me to polish his brown shoes. I said my father was in the mosque and would polish them as soon as he came back but I decided that this was an easy thing to do so I cleaned his shoes myself, only I used black polish by mistake. When the man returned he was furious and slapped me twice in the face and said my father would now have to buy him a new pair of shoes. I ran to the mosque and told my father what had happened and said he had to talk to the man. My father tried to cool him down saying I was just a child which must have worked because the man took his shoes, which my father had re-polished, and left.

My father asked if my face hurt and I said it was not as bad as my religious teacher and we both started laughing. Then my father began crying and he said from that day I should stop cleaning shoes because it was a poor job and no one would respect me if I did that all my life. He wanted me to qualify as a cycle mechanic but I really wanted to be a TV engineer because I had seen all the films and Tom and Jerry cartoons on TVs in a shop near our stand. I suppose it seemed somehow more glamorous to me, but I could not say anything to my father who gave me 5 rupees to buy something for myself and go straight home.

I bought a few bags of crisps for my little brothers who were so excited by them, but my mom asked me why I had come home early. I told her what had happened and she held me in her lap and started crying. I said that my dream now was to become a TV and radio engineer not just a bicycle mechanic and she had to tell my father because I was too frightened to go against his wishes.

When he came home that evening she told him and he readily agreed saying he knew of two TV mechanics in the area and both were from Pakistan. The next day we went to see them and one agreed to take me on as an apprentice on the condition that I cleaned the shop every day and made tea for the staff. My father reassured him that I was a hard worker and would do everything he asked.

In a few months I had learned a lot and my salary had risen to 200 rupees a week. Also, the shopkeeper advised me to learn English so I could understand the TV manuals. I was a quick learner and already had picked up Pashto, mostly from playing marbles with the Pakistani children, I could read and speak Farsi, or Dari as we call it, and I had learned Urdu from watching a lot of Indian movies on television.

My boss was a good man and treated me like a son. Every time he opened up a TV he told me to sit next to him and learn what he was doing, looking at the sound system, the power supply and the condensers. In other words practical step-by-step lessons on how a television worked. To help me learn English – albeit American English – he sent me to a centre with 300 rupees which was enough for one course, one hour a day every day for nearly a year; it was half an hour's bicycle ride away. It was hard work, particularly trying to master the English grammar, but by the end I could read and write well enough to understand the complicated manuals.

One day I was riding my bike to my English lesson when I stopped at traffic lights and someone called my name. I looked up; it was a Suzuki car and inside was my old head teacher. She was wearing a face covering which she removed and asked where I was going. I pointed at my books and said I had given up school because all the subjects were in Pashto but I was now studying English because I wanted to become a TV and radio engineer. She said I was different to all her other students and the teachers talked about me every day. She wished me good luck and said she was sure I would achieve happiness one day in my life because I was already thinking like a mature man.

Sadly my boss developed leg cancer and lost one of his legs which meant he was too ill to come into the shop every day so he asked me to run the business in his absence. If I really got stuck on a job he would come in and help, but I was left in charge in return for 20 per cent of everything the shop made as he had to pay all the running costs.

Before long I was making 300 rupees a day which made a huge difference to the family. My mom was struggling to cope at home as I was working full time and not collecting the wood and coal for cooking, a chore which had now passed to my brother, Ahmed. But I said that was no longer necessary as I was earning enough to buy the wood from a big warehouse and, instead of scavenging on the streets, I tried to help my brothers, teaching them what I could because they didn't stay long in school either. Ahmed eventually became a tailor and I brought Nur to be with me in the shop so he didn't get into trouble on the streets until I could teach him how to become a TV engineer himself.

However, the fighting and the impact of the war were never far away. My aunt's husband, Rafe, who had been a commander in the Communist Afghan army fighting against the Mujahideen, realised that when the fighting reached Jalalabad Afghanistan was no longer a safe place for him and his wife and they had come to stay secretly with us in Peshawar, initially living in the same room as us. It was all too crowded and he eventually bought a tent and lived in the courtyard with the others. But he never dared to go out on the streets in case he was recognised by other refugees as the man who had fought against the Mujahideen. They eventually found out where he was staying and they warned my father that if he ever left our compound he would be killed. His wife would go out to do their shopping and he would send me from time to time to buy his cigarettes.

My father told him that he could not spend the rest of his life hiding in his tent and he would have to find a job. My uncle, Ghulam Haidar, who had been a top commander with the Mujahideen, spoke to some senior people and said Rafe now realised what he had done was wrong but that he had only been fighting for his country and trying to make some money just as those who had fought with the Mujahideen had joined to make money themselves. My uncle said Rafe now regretted what he had done and was praying every day to make amends, which wasn't true because I never saw him praying, and could he now be pardoned to get on with his life? He was forgiven and allowed to get on with his life again. He said he hoped the Mujahideen would eventually bring peace to Afghanistan.

My life had almost taken a different turn when a colleague in our TV shop who was ten years older than me said he intended to start a new life in Dubai as there was no future in Afghanistan; Pakistan was getting worse and he tried to convince me to join him. He had a lot of skills and was actually a master tailor and had taught my brother, Ahmed, how to sew. He told me that he had relatives who owned a warehouse in Dubai where he was going to work and he would see if there was a similar job for me. The problem was I needed 40,000 rupees for a visa. I had been saving about 200 rupees a week secretly from my family as my parents were getting old and I would need to be able to afford to give them a proper burial.

After a few months my friend contacted me from Dubai to say he had found a job for me as a TV mechanic; by then I had saved enough for a visa and went to the consul in Peshawar where I found the Taliban sitting there recording people's names and the first thing they asked was why I didn't have a full beard. I explained that I was still young and my beard was still growing – there were a lot of people who were refused permission to travel because their beards were not long enough which seemed a strange way to make any decision.

But the official also wanted to know if I was running away from Pakistan and Afghanistan and I said I just wanted to visit a relative. He seemed satisfied although he said I could not just put my name as Tella in the passport and insisted it should be Tallah Tella. What I didn't know was that many of the educated people from Kabul were simply going to the UNHCR office and claiming asylum and being allowed free entry to places like Canada and Australia after just a few months of applying and even being given a free airline ticket.

Nevertheless I faxed my passport details to my friend in Dubai; it was my first legitimate ID which I was so proud of that I carried it around everywhere. This was going to be a new life and I would be able to send good money back to support my family at home. But almost the very day he received my details Dubai announced that they would not admit any more Afghan citizens because of the Taliban regime. My money was wasted and I threw away my passport with the phoney name.

Politically Afghanistan was still in turmoil. In 1992 Najibullah had been thrown out of office and his government toppled. He had wanted to hand over power to Hekmatyar but the other leaders, including Ahmad Shah Massoud, did not want Hekmatyar in Kabul, so an agreement was reached with the former communist Afghan army generals. Civil war was inevitable and yet with Najibullah gone we had begun thinking about returning home. America wanted peace and above all it wanted to get back some of the weaponry including Stinger missiles which were valued at around $8,000 by the fighters. My uncle had about ten himself and I remember telling him that he would be rich if he handed them over, but he refused.

Its first initiative having failed, the US enlisted the help of Pakistan's ISI and a man called Haji Ayub Afridi, said to be the founder of the Afghan heroin trade. Mullah Mohammad Omar formed a new group under the auspices of the Pakistan government in 1994. It was called the Taliban and consisted initially of just a handful of students, hence its name. Years later the Prime Minister of Pakistan, Imran Khan, would acknowledge that his country was responsible for creating the Taliban.

We, of course, had been following the events glued to the single television I had put up in our little compound in Peshawar and wondering what the Taliban could do for us. We decided to return to Afghanistan because we thought the Taliban would get rid of Al Qaeda, we would no longer have the Arabs in the streets and peace would return because we regarded the Taliban as angels, but we didn't know their secret plans and then their extreme punishments for breaking their rules. Yes, we understood that Sharia law was being introduced and, even if that meant not shaving, the men in the compound felt it was better than life in effective exile where we weren't even popular. People in Peshawar were saying why didn't we go back to our own country because we were taking their jobs. Children would shout abuse at us in the streets and even the Pakistani police would stop us on any pretext, take our money then release us. We had no official documents so life was difficult – we were simply not welcome anymore. While I may have found this attitude hard at the time, I now see it happening everywhere as refugees and even ordinary migrants from around the world are prepared to put up with anything and risk everything, even their own lives, in search of a better life.

It was particularly hard for me because returning to Afghanistan meant giving up my job. When I told my shopkeeper that I had to go, he offered to adopt me but I refused to change my nationality and, in any case, my father needed me to support the family. When he saw my mind was made up he came to the shop one morning with a box of tools for me worth at least 5,000 rupees which he said was to help me set up my own business. He said I had been very honest and never stolen money so he wanted to help. Later he and his wife came to visit our home to wish us well saying he was confident I could now run a business on my own.

Once we had decided to leave someone advised my father to go to the UN office and register that we were no longer refugees and would be leaving to start up again in Kushgumbad. The UN office paid us $2,000 to help us start anew which would later prove to be very useful. Shortly afterwards we put all our belongings in a lorry and, instead of going across the mountains, we went by main road. Despite the long queues of lorries heading in the same direction as each one was being checked by the Pakistani military in case we had been hiding weapons, the drive back to Jalalabad only took just over two hours, a far cry from the 15-day trek we had made across the mountains nearly ten years earlier.

SEVEN

Taliban raid

The lorry driver dropped us off in Jalalabad City instead of going directly to our village because not only was the road home very bad, but the driver was scared that he might be attacked by armed gangs, lose his lorry or even be kidnapped. Everyone on the streets seemed to be carrying guns and ready to use them. So he simply dumped all our belongings at the lorry service station where we could see a huge refugee camp full to overflowing. It was as though we were still in Pakistan but my father said these were all people who had fled the fighting in Kabul and could not get to Pakistan. Even Jalalabad itself was not that peaceful. The Taliban were racing around in their 4x4s bristling with guns, demanding that people should be praying in the mosques; in some cases people said they had already prayed but were told to go back in the mosque so the Taliban could actually see them praying. Sometimes they would stop people in the street and measure the length of their beards by grasping them in their fists; if they were not long enough the men were arrested and ordered to grow them longer. I began wondering what was really happening.

Towards the end of 1994 we had great hope that the Taliban would not touch us and may even have been beneficial. Actually my main concern was having to grow a beard but I reasoned that it would only be for a short time, the rules would be relaxed and I could even save a little money by not having to buy blades for my razor.

As our home had been destroyed we went to stay with some relatives in the city but they were not happy about all our belongings piled up in front of their house, so we decided after a few days to go back to our village and, hopefully, even if just one room was still standing, we could live there and slowly rebuild our home.

My father hired a donkey and cart and loaded all our bags and parcels. I didn't think the poor donkey could pull it all and said I was happy to walk even if it took two or three hours. Taliban passed us in cars firing their guns in the air at nothing in particular and I was full of regret about leaving Pakistan, but I could not say anything to my father as he had clearly been in a hurry to return home and, in any case, he was head of the family.

When we reached our village I saw my parents crying because they were back in their village for the first time in so many years, but also I am sure because they were upset at the state of our home. I wondered why we had decided to come back to this life without shelter, electricity or water. I even thought of running away and going back to Pakistan where my old boss had offered to adopt me, but at the same time I had to think about what would happen to the family.

Ninety per cent of the village had been destroyed and we found just three walls of our own home standing and even the heavy wooden gate had been stolen. I actually saw some of these gates in a shop when I came to live in the UK some years later. The shopkeeper said a film company had once bought half the contents of Afghan items – carpets and antiques – to lend authenticity to a movie they were making. He couldn't have known the sadness I felt at such looting; these were not antiques, they were part of our homes.

We quickly rebuilt one room and, when we had completed a second, my uncle, Haidar, who had ended up polishing shoes in Pakistan after doing *jihad*, came with his family to stay. He was very poor and my father said it was the least he could do for his own brother, but it was all very cramped.

The arguments started immediately with my mom telling my father that he should first have come alone to Kushgumbad and seen the situation for himself before moving the whole family from Peshawar where we were far better off.

We were not alone in returning. Other families who had come back had already started rebuilding, but we also found strangers who had put up houses near the river; they were like gypsies building in the bushes where the Mujahideen used to hide from the Russians, but there was nothing anyone could do about it as the original village elders had died and no one was in charge.

I asked my father what I should do as we had lost most of our land and we had no animals to manage. This set my father off again cursing our luck. It was a tragedy, he said, that the Russians had come, but the Mujahideen had started the *jihad* and this is what had happened to our home. The Russians were not interested in our villages; indeed they had built the olive factory, a sugar factory and many bridges. What had the Mujahideen brought – destruction – and that, he reminded us all, was exactly what he had warned everyone about years earlier. This, of course, was followed by Al Qaeda and then the Taliban and later still Daesh. As my father used to say, the parent is Mujahideen, the children become Taliban, their nephews Daesh and the grandchildren will become something else. A donkey is a donkey, he would repeat again and again; you can change the way it looks with different rugs but underneath it remains a donkey.

I said to my father there was no point arguing about what had happened in the past; we should think about the future and how we could earn some money as we didn't have any land or animals to look after, and the only way we could do that was by going to Jalalabad where he could polish shoes and I would try and get a TV mechanics job.

He agreed and set up his stand outside an old friend's shop cleaning shoes while I offered my services as a professional TV mechanic. I found a shop where the owner needed an assistant but first he wanted to test my ability. Not only was it obvious that I knew what I was doing, but it was also clear to me that he made a lot of mistakes when he was trying to repair TVs himself. When I pointed them out he was a bit embarrassed as I quickly showed him how to fix a Russian TV. He could see I was fully qualified and he agreed a 50:50 split in the business.

But gradually the Taliban banned music, radios, TV and films, and would rip the tapes from cassettes and hang them up in the street. We knew that if they had found out what we were doing we would be in danger even though we could hear them playing music in their cars as they drove around. To disguise what our business was we stacked cardboard boxes in the front window hoping that they would soon give up the destruction. But we saw more and more Arabs from Al Qaeda with their long turbans and beards coming to our villages and walking about freely. The Taliban said nothing but the Mujahideen were very upset, although that didn't stop some of the Mujahideen joining the Taliban because they had no other way of making money; they were fighters and had no other skill.

Women, of course, had to wear burqas, were banned from going to school and were not even allowed to walk alone in the street without being accompanied by a man. They started stopping all cars, removing the radios and cassette players, tearing out the cables and smashing the equipment on the ground. I thought of collecting them all up and sending them to Pakistan for repair to make a bit of money but that would have been too risky. This was a very bad time.

Meanwhile my sister, Wahida, was born but there was no celebration – poor girl, she just increased the numbers living in a single room.

The whole culture of Jalalabad was changing, the sense of freedom and opportunity. It used to be something of a tourist destination with people from the cold north in Kabul coming to visit every year in the winter months because it was warmer and in the hot summer days the rich people from Jalalabad would visit the north. Pashtun and Tajiks would intermarry, and every year on Independence Day from Britain we had three days' holiday. Big screens would be put up in Jalalabad so people could watch movies in the open air, there would be dancing and a lot of famous singers would come and perform. My father would hold me on his shoulders to see the sights; it was a great celebration.

But all that joy stopped. The culture also changed with the arrival of new people speaking Arabic to each other and even the way people prayed soon changed, an influence brought in by the Wahabis which very quickly resulted in animosity between ordinary Muslims and the more extreme Wahabis. Our elders would argue with them: what are you doing, why are you praying like this? There were arguments everywhere in Jalalabad.

More strangers kept arriving in our village and increasing the number of new houses. The original mosque had been demolished but in the new one we even started seeing a lot of gunmen; they would lean their Kalashnikovs against the wall and start praying without any trace of shame at the killing and abuse they were carrying out. My father would say to them: "You came here for *jihad* but now *jihad* is over you should go back to your own country." They said "No, this is our land because in Islam there are no borders and no countries." It was not how I imagined life in my village would be.

In 1997 my brother, Faiz, was born at home, but even with two rooms it was overcrowded for both families. We all prayed that one day things would improve and we might even get electricity, but at least we had a hand pump for water instead of having to go to the river every day because the UN had helped us dig a well.

The strange thing was that we used to get visitors from Jalalabad who wanted to admire the views of the river and countryside. I, at least, saw our village as a place to escape from and here were people treating it as a sightseeing break. The women didn't cover their faces and my father warned them to wear a veil because there would be trouble if the Taliban arrived and found them dressed in that way.

I had been in business for three years when my boss decided to leave for Pakistan to seek a new life. He said if I could give him 100,000 Pakistani rupees the shop would be mine completely. I could only offer 50,000 rupees paying 30,000 immediately and the balance when I had managed to save or borrow some more. He acknowledged that the business had grown thanks to my expertise winning customers from rival shops. So I wrote a letter making a formal agreement that he had sold his shop because somehow I knew that something might happen and I wouldn't have proof of our deal without it. He signed the letter and exactly six months later came back, probably because he could not find work, saying he would return my money and I had to hand over the shop. I refused saying I respected him as my teacher but we had a deal. I had paid him money and now I could pay him the outstanding balance. There was a man who ran a cutlery shop who had been a witness to the agreement and told me not to accept and that he and his friends would support me. When we had made the deal my boss had said something at the time that made me suspicious. He accepted the deal but had warned that he might return and then we would need to talk. When I had insisted on the formal agreement he asked me if I didn't trust him, but I said it was not a question of trust, just good business.

I called a meeting of my neighbours and I told them what he wanted. I said I would only agree if he paid me 150,000 rupees because the business had now grown. All the neighbours backed me and said if he had any complaints he could go and talk to the Taliban. I paid him the extra 20,000 rupees and he left. He was not happy and did not speak to me for a long time although he opened another shop in Jalalabad far away from my premises which didn't do very well.

By now I was the richest boy in the village and could afford to buy my own bicycle. I got Nur to sit with me because he wasn't going to school and I hoped to teach him how to become a TV mechanic himself; at least that would keep him off the streets and away from trouble with the other kids. Ahmed meanwhile was working as a tailor's apprentice. I was constantly thinking about their future because I was effectively supporting the whole family; my father was still polishing shoes but was not earning much money. I remember Nur saying to me once that we should make our father stay at home because it was embarrassing for us that he polished shoes for a living and his friends were teasing him about it. I said we don't have any land and if our father went home he would get sick. We should be proud of him. I told him that one day I might not be able to be a mechanic and I would have to go back to polishing shoes myself as I had done before when I also had to collect scrap paper and cans from the street, so he shouldn't be so proud.

That change in our fortunes happened sooner than expected. One day I was sitting in my shop working on 10 or 15 televisions, all still hidden behind boxes with a little gap so people could come in, when suddenly I saw a car stop right in front of the entrance. Men got out all armed to the teeth with their turbans and long beards; they were all chewing on *naswar* – a popular form of tobacco or snuff. I remember my boss in the shop used to do the same then take it out and throw it away before wiping his hand on the wall which I had to clean off every day. Once he asked me to get some Coca Cola because a rich customer was coming. I didn't notice him dropping a piece of his *naswar* in my bottle and when I had a drink I fell on the floor unconscious it was so strong.

The visit from the Taliban was more serious. I stood up as two men came in because I knew this meant trouble and wanted to show some respect. One of them started speaking Urdu which I immediately didn't like because it showed that he was a Pakistani Taliban. They wanted to rule our village, our country, our whole lives. I must have been feeling brave because I asked him why he didn't take his Sharia laws to his own country; why did he want to inflict it on us.

He told me my business was *haram,* or un-Islamic, and I should know that. He and his men had been ordered to break everything up because my business was supporting music and dancing. Nur was sitting looking at him shaking. I said what I did was not against Islam; if it was, why did we have it before when Afghanistan had had Islamic governments for hundreds of years. The Taliban were just imposing their own ideas. I said he did not speak my language and my business was not *haram.* As I argued he picked up his Kalashnikov with a bayonet shouting how dare I speak to him like that and he was now going to take my eyes out. Thank God there was a big table between us because I was able to put my arm up to my face. As he lunged forward the bayonet slashed my forearm and glanced off digging into my head.

Blood starting pouring all over me, Nur was screaming and I thought I was going to die. I believe it was another Arab Taliban who pulled the Pakistani back. Then the driver rushed in and said why was he trying to kill me; they were only supposed to break everything. They managed to cool my attacker down and got him back into their car then they returned and set about smashing all the televisions throwing them on the floor. The other shopkeepers had closed their shutters; nobody dared to come to my help or even look to see what was happening although they must have heard the noise. I was shaking and bleeding and thought I was going to die. When they had broken all the televisions they sped off.

I looked around at what remained of my shop then grabbed Nur, jumped in a passing rickshaw and headed home. First the rickshaw rider said he would take me to hospital but I refused in case there were other Taliban there who would simply hit me again. We got as close to our village as the rickshaw could go and we ran the rest of the way home, stumbling on the rough path as I was so dizzy from the loss of blood. Nur was crying, too young to understand what was going on and why we had been attacked.

I told my mom what had happened and she quickly burned some clothes and put the ashes on my wounds as we had no other medicine and, of course, I had no stitches. As she treated my wounds I remember complaining that we should never have come to Jalalabad.

I had to rest for about three months as I kept falling over whenever I tried to stand up and needed a stick to support myself. However, I slowly recovered and returned to salvage what I could from the shop but everything had been taken, even my tools down to the last screwdriver had been stolen. I went to other radio shops looking for work but they were all closed down. Even if people had little transistor radios playing in shops they would hide them away when Taliban patrols were near. The shopkeepers said I was lucky because they had killed so many people in Jalalabad; some had even been hanged in public. I asked what we should do and they said they were just praying for a miracle. It was up to the Mujahideen to resist the Taliban otherwise they would destroy the whole country. But nothing happened and before long the Taliban had taken control of Kabul and other towns.

Starting up my business again was out of the question, but as I recovered gradually people who knew I was a TV and radio mechanic came to our village and brought their radios and tape-recorders, which they had kept secretly, for me to repair. I told them I only had a few basic tools but they asked me to do what I could. They thought that as it was my village nobody would care and the Taliban would never know. Some of my old customers whose televisions had been smashed in my shop came round demanding compensation but I told them it was not my fault and if they had any complaints they should go and speak to the Taliban.

I needed to do something to earn some money as my father was making so little polishing shoes. I decided not to touch TVs because I didn't have the necessary tools and we didn't have electricity but I could fix radios and tape recorders. So I began work in a corner of our room and tried to keep the children away from the equipment. I remember when my sister, Saida, was born in 1998 she would make a lot of noise and it was difficult for me to adjust the filters in the radios so I had to ask my mom to try and keep her quiet.

I carried on working like this for about six months, then one evening another group of Taliban arrived at my house. I think the driver may have been the same one who came to my shop. They burst in which set everyone off shouting and crying. My mom grabbed the baby and screamed at them thinking they were thieves, but they could see exactly what I was doing. I thought if they didn't kill me in the shop they would surely kill me now. They said I was a non-believer, started swearing at me and beating me. My father tried to stop them but they carried on and more than 30 years later I still have back pain from my injuries.

They pushed my father out of the way and dragged me and Ahmed out of the house. I was expecting to be shot at any moment and tried telling them that we only listened to the Koran on the radio, but they didn't believe me. The children were all screaming and my mom was shouting demanding to know where they were taking us. They said we were going to Jalalabad prison. I have no doubt that someone in the village who was sympathetic to the Taliban betrayed me. How else would they have known what I was doing because they never normally went into people's private homes?

We were pushed into a cell with about 35 other prisoners with no facilities. Ahmed was crying constantly which annoyed the others as well as the guards so much that he was released the next day and told to make his own way home.

For the rest of us it was a terrifying ordeal. Each night they dragged people out of the cell seemingly at random, then I heard shooting and the prisoner never came back. We were all wondering if it would be our turn next. I thought about my family and wondered if this really was how my life would end. There was no way I or any of the other prisoners could escape; it just seemed that we would have to sit and wait for our turn and yet for some reason I didn't give up hope. There was no logic to it but I remembered my teacher who seemed to have confidence in me and maybe that helped me even when the guards threw open the door and snatched another prisoner out. The strange thing was there was no resistance from the poor victim. Perhaps they thought that somehow, for some reason, they had been pardoned, but we all knew when we heard the gun shot.

One night they dragged me out and the guard told me not to speak. I could hardly walk as I was so terrified and shaking. When you are facing certain death your legs don't work and I was sure they would shoot me at any second. So many things raced through my mind; I wondered how the family would cope, how they would find my dead body and get it home for burial. But the guard then told me not to worry as my uncle was waiting outside. He said I was being released on condition I would never be seen in Afghanistan again; if I was I would be shot on the spot. He told me to go through the gates and turn left and left again where my uncle was waiting. It was pitch dark and I didn't dare look back. I didn't believe a word the guard had said and I was waiting for the bullet in the back of my head.

I carried on walking into the darkness until I heard my uncle calling me. He put me on the crossbar of his bicycle and pedalled away quickly. I had been in the prison for more than a month and it turned out that my family had been trying all that time to find a guard they could trust to bribe. In the end they had to pay $3,000 which included the $2,000 from the UN relief fund to rebuild our lives.

It was early morning when we finally reached home and the sun was still not up. No sooner had my parents hugged me and welcomed me home than my uncle said I would have to leave immediately because if the Taliban found me in the morning I would be shot. I asked where I should go and he said Pakistan where my aunt lived. I actually thought thank God because it was where I wanted to go and at least now my father would not stop me; I hoped I would be able to resume my work as a TV mechanic with my former boss. My mom collected some of my clothes together and put them in a plastic bag, my father handed me a little money, I gave everyone a last hug and left.

My uncle took me to the bus stop outside our village where there were a few other people waiting. He asked the driver to take me to Torkham border between Pakistan and Afghanistan and I climbed on the top of the bus even though there were plenty of seats inside because I wanted to look back at my village and the mountains as the sun rose. I somehow knew that I would probably never see my home again; once more I was fleeing my country with no ID and just a little money to become a refugee.

When we reached the border crossing I attached myself to a group of women who thought it was a bit odd, but I knew the guards were unlikely to stop a young boy that they would assume was part of a family; fortunately my hair covered the big scar in my head so that did not raise any suspicions and we were just waved across the border, no questions asked, into Pakistan. The militia there did wonder where I was going and when I said I was returning to my home they assumed I was a refugee.

Others did take an interest in me but not for security reasons. I was walking alone and went to the kind of small restaurants people were visiting for lunch and dinner. The rich people were sitting inside the restaurant and ordering fresh hanging lamb while the ordinary people were eating outside the restaurant on the floor ordering *chapli* kebab and kidney, a popular street food; the smell is so nice and the taste delicious. But I had very little money and I sat on the ground next to the cooker and ordered what I could afford.

I soon realised that some men were looking at me very strangely, as they might look at a girl. I put my head down and started eating my food quickly when a man sat down next to me and asked where I was going? I said it was none of his business but I was waiting for my uncle who would soon be there and together we were going to Peshawar. He started laughing and told me I was handsome and if I wanted to be his bodyguard he would pay me 2,000 rupees a month. I refused and told him I was from Afghanistan and that my uncle was a Hezb-e-Islami commander. I said he should be ashamed of himself looking for gay boys as he was a Muslim. In fact most of the Pashtun tribal people proudly keep handsome boys aged 14 or 15 as their so-called bodyguards; it seems to be part of their culture.

But I was very scared and luckily he went away even though others were looking at me in a different way. I quickly finished my food and ran towards the bus station to catch the lorry to get to Peshawar as fast as I could because I knew I could easily be kidnapped by these tribal people.

As we drove away I believed I would never set foot in Afghanistan again.

EIGHT

People traffickers

Once across the border I took another bus that was really a converted lorry which even had seats on the roof, and travelled along a twisty road from Torkham to Landi Kothal and from there to Karkhano, a market area on the western side of Peshawar. It was unbelievable – everyone was walking around with guns and shops were openly selling cocaine. The Pakistan militia, which are like a tribal militia although not part of the Pakistan army or police, seemed to be in charge. These people stayed at the border in the customs area and operated independently of Pakistan law. They would search your belongings to see what people might be smuggling such as expensive clothes. They didn't always seize the goods; instead, they would bribe people to allow them to keep the items. It was almost lawless although everyone seemed to know what they could and could not get away with before carrying on their way.

Karkhano is on the edge of the Khyber Pass and to get to my aunt's house I had to take another lorry ride into Peshawar itself. My aunt wasn't expecting me and was stunned to see me standing at her door. She hugged me and, fearing the worst, immediately asked what had happened, why was I in Peshawar, how was the family and a hundred other questions. I said everything and everyone was fine apart from me but first I needed to rest. However, when she saw the scars on my head and arm she insisted I told her everything because she said she had high blood pressure and could not relax until she heard exactly what had happened. I explained how I had been attacked and imprisoned, how my family had bribed a guard to release me and how I had been forced to leave Afghanistan because my life was in danger. She was not surprised because she had warned my father so many times not to go back to his village as it was not safe but he had ignored her. And then, at last, I was able to rest and slept for I don't know how many hours.

The next day, a Friday, I went to pray in the mosque but it was full of Taliban, and the imam was only preaching about how important it was to recruit more fighters for the Taliban to send them to do *jihad* in Afghanistan as it was our duty, and that Sharia law had to be imposed in Pakistan; they wanted to overturn the old British colonial law. These messages, which had nothing to do with religion, were being broadcast daily across the city from loudspeakers. I just knew I could not stay there forever as it was the headquarters of the Taliban along with Quetta in Balochistan where all the leaders were based. There was a constant two-way stream of refugees; the old communist Afghan senior command, like my aunt's husband, General Rafe, was heading into Pakistan and the pro-Mujahideen followers were travelling in the opposite direction. It was madness.

My first priority was to try and find a job as I needed to pay my aunt something towards my keep and if I had anything left over I wanted to send money to help support my family at home in Kushgumbad. I went back to the shop where the owner had offered to adopt me but sadly he had died and the shop had been sold to someone who didn't recognise me and, as he already had plenty of staff, there was no room for me anyhow. I found another shop owner who did remember me and, after I had told him what had happened, he offered me a job. But he warned me that even in Peshawar the mullahs were telling him not to play music loudly, although they couldn't close the business down because we were under Pakistan law. The Taliban influence was obvious and we could see the youngsters who began believing everything these teachers were saying were growing their beards long, going to mosques and becoming more radicalised.

My aunt and the general had two children; the younger one was taken to hospital for a vaccination but his leg got infected and had to be removed, then a short time later he died. Incredibly exactly the same thing happened to his older brother, Zyarmal, who also lost a leg having been infected by the vaccination although he survived. My aunt and her husband decided not to have any more children.

Years later when my sister, Wahida, was older she married Zyarmal although I didn't really approve as they were closely related, but my aunt pleaded with me to agree. They now have four children of their own and live with my mom as my aunt and her husband both died quite young within three months of each other. They had had a tough life. The general had been reduced to clearing tables in a restaurant earning just 50 rupees a day and bringing home whatever scraps the customers had left behind. If there were no leftovers he would come home empty-handed. The Pakistani owners didn't care because they knew most of the Afghan refugees were desperate for any money they could get.

However, my aunt and her husband were happy to have me to stay. They treated me like their son, and I could help them buy a few extras with my earnings, although there was never enough left over to send anything home to my family and, in any case, there were no direct connections to transfer money to our village. The only contact I had with my family was when relatives visited Peshawar and gave me some news because we didn't have a phone. Life was hard for my parents too as fighting continued between rival Taliban groups and the ex governor of Jalalabad, Haji Qader, as well as the Mujahideen. Basic facilities were still non-existent and it says a great deal about the lack of development in rural Afghanistan by 2000 that some places still had no electricity or running water.

Although I had a job, I never stopped thinking about how I could get out of Peshawar because the Taliban were recruiting all the time and it was not safe for anyone who opposed them; if they discovered any former communist Afghan army officers like my aunt's husband they would be killed.

General Rafe could see I was not happy and told me if I wanted to escape from these people I should try and leave the country. He said he would have done so himself but he could never afford the cost of getting to Europe, legally or illegally. He said I had to convince my father to sell some of his land because with that money I could change my life forever. At the same time I wanted to go back and see my family one more time so I worked out a plan and started growing my beard long.

I decided that I had to return to my village secretly, disguised as a Taliban, because I needed to speak to my father in person; I couldn't send one of my cousins because he would never trust them with what I was about to ask. Once my beard was long enough and wearing the same clothes as the Taliban with turban and long scarf, I retraced my steps taking a lorry to Torkham, then to Jalalabad and from there I took a rickshaw and walked the rest of the way back to my village.

Everyone asked me: what had happened, why was I there, didn't I know how dangerous it was to be seen in the village as the Taliban were everywhere now. They quickly pulled me inside, and I sat with my father to explain why I had come.

I said as his eldest son I had always done my best to support the family but now my shop had been demolished. My father immediately warned me not to even think about going near the shop because I would be instantly recognised and in any case someone else had taken it over and was selling groceries.

I said I had no intention of going to Jalalabad but I needed him to do something for me. I said I planned to go back to Peshawar and open a much bigger shop repairing TVs and I was confident I could make 600 rupees a day but I needed to borrow some money off him which I promised to repay in two or three years. He asked how much I wanted and I said $10,000. He just laughed and asked if I was planning to open a warehouse but I explained that I wanted to buy a shop in central Peshawar where the prices were much higher and that I also planned to open a business selling TV and radio spare parts which I would acquire from Lahore and Karachi. I said I would become rich enough to move the whole family to Pakistan and I would buy a house in Peshawar. He thought I was dreaming but my mom convinced him that it was worth it because the land which he would borrow against was beginning to be washed away and soon it would be worthless as farmland.

He went to one of the tribal leaders and managed to borrow $8,000 against the property; the arrangement was if the loan was paid back within six months he would get the deeds back. My father reminded me that the land originally belonged to my grandfather and so it was important that one day he would get it back in family hands.

The money was all in bundles of notes which I wrapped round my legs and hid behind my back under my shirt, and early the next morning I caught another lorry back having said my last goodbye to the family for the second time.

I was terrified in case I was searched and the money was found, and I prayed some chapters from the Koran over and over again in my head to keep me safe. By chance only my bag was searched by the Taliban who stopped us but my heart was pounding; luckily my simple disguise seemed to work and they never asked me where I was from or to see any form of ID.

Needless to say I had no intention of opening any TV repair shops – I needed the money to pay people traffickers. My uncle had assured me that by offering to pay them so much my passage would be safe and guaranteed. When I got back to Peshawar I didn't even show the money to my aunt but I told her husband that I had managed to get the cash and now he had to find someone to help me and by that I meant track down an agent who would put me in direct contact with the traffickers. But that wasn't difficult because there were so many in Peshawar as there are today; you just had to hope the one you picked was reliable.

A meeting was arranged in Karkhano where an agent had a money-changing business but his real profits came through his role as a people trafficker's agent. He looked at me as though he was trying to assess how I would cope with the dangers ahead then asked if I spoke Pashto, Urdu or Farsi. I said I spoke all three as well as English.

Apparently satisfied, he told me to deposit my money at a trusted bank in the bazaar and get a letter from them. The arrangement was that half the money would be paid up front and the balance would be released once I had reached my destination. We each had a copy of the letter to that effect and an agreement about where I was going. I really wanted to get to Canada but that would have cost me $15,000 which I didn't have, $8000 would get me as far as London or $5,000 to anywhere in Europe. I thought I better choose London because I spoke English. The agent then wrote another letter which I had to sign saying if I died, was kidnapped or drowned at sea the traffickers would not be held responsible for my death because they didn't want any trouble from my other family members. I began to realise just what I was undertaking and the risks involved.

He gave me his mobile number in case anything should happen to me but he told me to memorise the number and not write it down because he didn't want anyone to find his details on a piece of paper in my pocket should I get arrested. All I could now do was wait for their call at my shop or a neighbour's house.

A month went by and still I hadn't heard a word so I rang him to ask what was happening because I said I knew that another agent had managed to send three people to Europe in the meantime; it wasn't true but I wanted to hurry him up. I said I didn't know the name of the agent but he had definitely got three people away in the past week. He said not to worry because his people wanted to be sure I got to London safely and not to rush their plans.

In June I finally got a call telling me to go to the bazaar in Peshawar and buy some shirts, trousers and a leather briefcase to make me look like a businessman; I was also told to shave off my beard just leaving a moustache. They then made me a Pakistani ID card and a fake Pakistani passport with a new name, Nosher Khan. They said I would be convincing because my accent was just like the people from Peshawar. Armed with my false documents and my new name I was sent to the Iranian consulate in Peshawar to ask for a tourist visa. As anticipated they asked why I planned to visit Iran and I said I wanted to see the holy shrine of of Imam Reza, a descendant of the prophet Muhammad. I returned three days later and they had stamped my passport with a short stay three-month visa – it was the only legitimate part of my documentation.

They sent me and the two other illegal immigrants by car into Balochistan; it was a long journey through the desert and the driver kept falling asleep so I had to jolt him to wake him up. He asked me if I could drive but I didn't have a licence. We were stopped a couple of times on the way before we finally reached Quetta where we were handed over to different agents. It was all a question of trust. We had no idea who we were meeting or what the plans were so we were totally in their care, but we had no alternative and had to go along with everything they said.

We spent two nights in Quetta, apparently waiting for the right guard to come on duty. When they knew his shift had started we had to move quickly so he could stamp our passports. We just walked into Iran without being challenged and found there were other agents waiting. They bundled us into a car and we set out on the 2,200 kilometres journey to Tehran. We were stopped a few times by Iranian checkpoints on the way but our Pakistani passports passed their casual glances and we were welcomed. If for one moment they had suspected we were Afghans we would probably have been shot. The guards spoke Farsi which, of course, I could understand but I had been warned not even to say hello in Farsi and pretended not to understand keeping quiet because I knew this was a critical moment for me. The mullahs in Iran imposed very strict laws and if they had thought for a moment that I was an illegal immigrant travelling on fake documents I would have been in trouble.

We arrived in a suburb of Tehran called Khayban Amir Kabir where they had rented rooms for us in a hotel. We didn't have to pay anything; I only had $400 on me and I didn't want to spend it. It was the first time I had ever slept in a proper bed. It was luxury – electricity and running water – and a lady came and made our beds every day and offered to clean our clothes. I remember thinking what has happened to our country where we don't have these facilities and yet Iran has gone through a revolution and the streets are all clean, the buildings are clean and people are so friendly. But I was missing my family and heartbroken at leaving them so while I was living in luxury I couldn't really enjoy it. I would go to the lounge where there was a big TV screen and watch Iranian movies, football and dancing. The food was free three times a day and I was able to wander about casually in the parks, all the time trying to memorise where my hotel was, and I was able to chat to some of the elderly people and discuss what terrible things were happening in Afghanistan without fear of reprisal or betrayal.

I went to the Grand Bazaar where the girls and boys were walking about freely together and I saw boys openly smoking hashish and cannabis. I thought perhaps I should stay here and get my uncle to cancel all the plans to move me to London, but then I realised there was no future for me in Iran; it may have seemed free and easy but I knew the mullahs were in charge which was too like the extreme Taliban at home in Afghanistan.

I must have spent a few weeks in the hotel wondering if I would ever leave when I heard on the news that Ahmad Shah Massoud, the hero of the Afghan people who had fought against the Soviet invasion and later Al Qaeda and the Taliban, had been assassinated in a suicide bombing by two people posing as TV journalists on 9 September 2001. It was terrible news but in one sense I thought it might help me when I tried to claim asylum as I could say they had killed my leader. Most of the Iranians were crying; even the hotel owner was crying and saying there was going to be trouble because they had killed the leader who had defeated the Taliban.

Two days later, however, 9/11 happened and I lost all hope. I was 22.

I called the mobile number I had been given from a telephone box and I said I didn't think I was ever going to leave as 9/11 had happened and security was going to be tightened and if they caught me with a fake passport they would accuse me of being with Al Qaeda and I would be killed.

He told me not to worry because their original plan had been to smuggle me out by land via Turkey but now I was going to be flown out so I should relax. I was paying good money and someone would soon come to the hotel and explain everything.

NINE

Arrival in France

Shortly after that call the agent himself travelled to Tehran and one night came to my room with a man he introduced as Mr Rana, describing him as the top people trafficker in Pakistan with a reputation of moving three or four hundred illegal immigrants every month. I have no idea if that was true or even if it was his real name but I was entirely in their hands – there was no going back. Mr Rana, which is a common name in India, was a Punjabi from Islamabad or Lahore, a very tall and a heavily built man, smartly dressed in Western clothes and accompanied by three beautiful Iranian women and another man. He was obviously successful at what he did. I was assured that Mr Rana was well connected around the world with contacts in America, Canada and Europe. What was certain was that this was a lucrative business for both of them with a regular flow of illegal immigrants ready to take a chance. There was a rumour that Mr Rana had once filled an entire plane with illegal immigrants he had such good contacts.

The other two people who had been staying with me in the hotel had simply disappeared one day before 9/11. They didn't tell me when they were going and in fairness I didn't want to get to know them better or even spend too much time sitting with them in case they gave me away. I never trusted them; in fact I was never sure whom I could trust.

The agent told me that today was my lucky day because they were going to issue me with a new visa, organise my flight and work out a new route to London. Mr Rana opened his bag, took out a fake Schengen visa, removed a sticker and told me to hold my passport open. He then got half a potato with some writing on it, stamped the visa and scribbled a signature on the imprint. The writing said: Italian Embassy, Islamabad.

I thought this was a very dangerous game. My whole future seemed to depend on how convincing a potato would appear to the authorities and I didn't think it would work because if I was caught they would be convinced I was one of the 9/11 supporters as all my paperwork was fake. I was not happy with what they had done, and I was young and scared. But Mr Rana reassured me that they would teach me exactly what to say at passport control and nothing would happen to me, but the only rule was I should never speak a single word of Farsi, even if they beat me and slapped me. While Farsi is the Iranian language it was, of course, also the language we spoke in Afghanistan, although we call it Dari. It would have been an instant giveaway and I would have been arrested.

Mr Rana patted me on the back saying I was so lucky because if someone had paid him $20,000 he wouldn't do this for them but now, instead of going by land, I would be flying to safety. He said he was only doing it for me because my uncle kept assuring the agent that if his nephew was delivered safely to London he had another 10 or 15 people waiting for him in the pipeline to make him even richer.

Mr Rana said I had to memorise some words and I was then given two hours of training. I was told that the next day I would be booked on a flight from Tehran airport but now I had to concentrate on what he was saying. In Tehran airport itself he had no contacts so it was both risky and very easy. Because 9/11 had happened security would definitely have been tightened but I wasn't to worry, just be brave. The first thing I had to do was to be sure to go to a counter where a woman not a man was checking tickets and passports. Secondly, when I reached the counter he would be standing in the background watching but from behind the glass. If anything happened to me and I was arrested they would know at once and would be able to find someone on the inside they could bribe quickly to get me released because if they took me to prison in central Tehran I would end up serving five or six years. The third thing I had to remember was to not even say hello in Farsi but just say a few words in English because then the lady would only question me in English because they didn't speak Urdu or Pashto. Mr Rana said if I tried to be clever and show I could speak Farsi I would be caught. I was to hand over my passport and casually look around and never directly in the lady's eyes. She would ask me where I was going and I should say Italy because my cousin was getting married there and I was going to spend two weeks on holiday before returning to Pakistan. She would also ask why I had chosen to fly from Iran to go to Italy and I had to say it was because Iran was my brother's country and I always hoped in my heart that one day I would be able to visit Imam Reza's Mosque. I was told this would make a good impression and I could add that I came from a poor family and when my father checked the cost of flights to Italy from Iran they were so cheap. If she asked where I got the Schengen visa from I should say I applied for it at the Italian Embassy in Islamabad. She wouldn't ask any more questions. I wrote all these instructions down precisely and memorised them word for word.

When I reached the airport I was amazed because these were exactly the questions the lady asked me, then she stamped my passport and said I was welcome. I looked back and the agent and Mr Rana just waved goodbye.

Then I wondered what I was supposed to do next, where should I sit and what should I wait for as I had never been in an airport departure lounge before. I didn't even know what I was supposed to do in an aeroplane. I showed my boarding pass to a security guard and, being sure to speak in broken English, asked where I was meant to go. The guard pointed out the gate and when the flight was called I was told where I had to sit according to my seat number.

The aeroplane was very scary and I didn't even dare to look out of the window because it was so high. I closed my eyes and couldn't believe that this was not all just a dream. At the same time I was shaking in case I got arrested; what should I do and what should I say? But they had told me not to worry because the flight would eventually take me all the way to Paris, France. This was the first time that I knew where I was going.

I had been booked on a flight from Tehran to Baku, Azerbaijan as the first leg of the journey but I still had no idea how I was going to end up in Europe. I didn't know anything about making flight connections and in Baku I didn't know how to go through passport control, but Mr

Rana again had told me not to worry because they had their own people in Azerbaijan and someone would come and help me.

When we arrived, everyone was streaming through the terminal towards the transfer desk and I was beginning to panic when I saw a very tall, unbelievably beautiful Russian lady army officer with three or four stars on her shoulders coming towards me. I thought for a moment I was about to be arrested as she walked straight up to me. Speaking in Russian, she asked: Nosher Kahn? I said yes and gave her my passport. She told me to sit in the coffee shop, take a newspaper and not to look around which was difficult as there were so many army personnel which made me nervous. She disappeared into an office and after five or ten minutes returned with a boarding pass which she put in my passport. She must have just printed it off because I never went to passport control or a check-in desk. She told me to wait until my flight to Paris was called and then she walked straight out of the airport – another of Mr Rana's contacts. Now at least I knew for the first time for sure how I was going to reach Europe.

My instructions on what I should do when we landed at Charles de Gaulle airport in Paris were equally precise. I should immediately move well away from the other passengers, find a toilet and wait there for two hours. On no account should I go straight to passport control. While I was waiting I had to wet my passport and boarding pass completely, tear them into tiny pieces and flush them away; Mr Rana and the agent had already taken my ID card. I did as I was told and flushed the toilet three or four times to be sure not a scrap of the documents remained. The reason for doing all this and for the delay in presenting myself to the authorities was that Mr Rana did not want them to know the route his illegal immigrants were using to get into the country.

I then went to immigration control and said I was from Afghanistan, I had no passport, no ticket and I was claiming asylum. It was almost a relief to be telling the truth for once but I had no idea what would happen next. They asked which airline I had flown on but I said I did not know as it was dark and all I knew was that it was a white aeroplane.

I was told to sit in a room with about ten other people they had also stopped that day – some Iraqi, some Iranian and some from Africa all of whom had arrived without passports. Like all refugees they were desperate, either anxious to escape a country where they felt their lives were at risk like me, or else simply to get a better life. I spoke to one of the Iranians who had been stopped and asked him why he was attempting to claim asylum as there was no fighting in Iran and what reason did he intend to give. He just laughed and said all the Iranians were claiming to be gay, which was outlawed in Iran. I later discovered that this was a very common reason given by Iranian asylum seekers so we now call all Iranians gay as a joke.

If I had stayed in Afghanistan I would definitely have joined up with Hekmatyar and the Mujahideen to fight against the Taliban because my life was being threatened, but I also would have wanted to fight for my country. My father would not have approved but you can't always do what your father tells you.

As for the agent who had set me up with Mr Rana, I heard that he had had a heart attack and died. He was only in his fifties but he was overweight. He had opened a jewellery shop; however, it was his side line in people trafficking that had made him a wealthy man. He and my uncle had built up a good relationship with all the people my uncle had pushed his way, paying my uncle a $500 commission each time and as a result the agent had even offered to traffic my uncle for free. But it never happened.

The immigration officers came and took us one by one for a strip search because as we were illegal immigrant they thought we might be smuggling drugs; it was so embarrassing because the police officers were ladies. I just said I was from Afghanistan and I had come to France because the Taliban had killed our leader, Massoud. They nodded saying they understood because Massoud was a friend of France; the only country Massoud had visited outside Afghanistan was France. During his stay in Paris he had warned the world that something terrible was going to happen unless the West helped his people in the fight against Al Qaeda. And, of course, he was proved right because 9/11 happened soon afterwards.

They then took us in a van to a detention centre where we found maybe 200 people all waiting for their cases to be heard. They gave us blankets, towels and free clothes with food three times a day. After a week in the centre a solicitor came and interviewed me. I was told I had a good case because they knew there was fighting in Afghanistan and so I had a golden opportunity to stay in France. They would give me all the documents I required to be a legal citizen so I could find a job. But there was no guarantee that I would get a permanent visa to remain in France and be granted French citizenship after four years, so I refused, saying I wanted to join my cousins in London. I also realised I didn't speak French and it would be hard for me to find work.

A few days later I was given a letter saying I had to leave France within 20 days but the document also gave me the right to travel for free on the trains and buses. They advised me, as they advised every refugee in the detention centre, to make my way to Calais, a place I had never heard of. They gave us all a map marking Calais and Dover, and even explained which train station to go to and told us to ask the security people to tell us which train to catch. Once we got to Calais we were told to find the refugee camp and from there just go and try our luck in getting to the UK. They knew exactly what we would try to do and it seemed that they just wanted to move us on as quickly as possible; once out of the detention centre and France, we were someone else's problem.

One evening, five or six of us were released but we split up as the others did not want to move about as a group. By the time I got to the station it was late at night and I had missed the last train to Calais. I found another three or four other migrants and we all spent the night huddled up outside the station. It was late September, very cold and we didn't have any money to buy food. During the night homeless people kept coming up to us trying to see what we had in our bags but we sent them away; I suppose they were in no better state than we were, but at least we had a plan.

Early the next morning, as commuters started arriving, three of us went back into the station, asked which platform we had to go to and showed our letters giving us free transport. The train took us all the way to Calais and from Calais station we walked for half an hour to the refugee camp.

We could see a lot of migrants from all over the world, trudging along the road, all desperate, all hoping for something better. When we got to the camp we lined up at the Red Cross centre and they took our details as we had no ID cards. I noticed that some of the migrants were giving their names in Farsi or Pashto saying their name was "Potato" or "Cucumber" or "Tree" which the officials were faithfully writing down having no idea what the words meant. I asked them why were they being silly and they said it was important not to give a real name otherwise when you get to England if they take your fingerprints and your name they will send you back to where you came from. I told them my name was Nosher Khan.

They gave three of us – all Afghans – a tent and told us to stay put until we were contacted again. We had to line up – more than 600 people – to get our food which was usually sandwiches and soup, twice a day. Human rights groups kept checking up on us giving vaccinations and handing out tablets when required.

This was our routine. I asked the others what I was supposed to do now. I could not just sit and wait for my name to be called from among all these people, and they said I had to try and get across the channel myself. They told me to join them and every night we and hundreds like us tried to hide on lorries, clambering under the lorry chassis or trying to break into the port. It was dangerous because if the driver had had to raise his wheels for any reason we would have been crushed to death.

But every night we tried and every night the dogs found us and we were arrested by the UK Border Agency police on the French side. They handed us over to the French police who put us in a van which was waiting until it was full with about 20 people. Then they drove about two kilometres away from the port until they were well out of sight of the UK Border Agency people, stopped the van, told us to get out and said in English: Good luck. Try again tomorrow. They didn't care and I am sure the last thing the detention centre wanted to see was van loads of illegal immigrants being returned every night.

It was a strange relationship between guard and migrant. One evening when we were being loaded back into the van, one of the guards shouted: "Assis!" which is French for "Sit down!". I tried out my French and repeated the word "Assis" but the guard hit me with his baton, I suppose because he thought I was mimicking him. But another black guard, who was just standing reading what I could see was a copy of the Koran, shouted at his colleague and they began arguing saying, I assumed, that he had no right to hit migrants and he was made to apologise. My fellow Muslim probably appreciated the plight of us migrants and knew there would be more of us the following night, so there was no point striking them. Nothing was going to change.

We kept trying to get on the lorries night after night and then we decided to board one of the ships directly by climbing over the high perimeter fences which were topped with razor wire. But despite my colleagues' efforts to help me I was too short and the last time I tried, I cut my hand badly. When the police caught us they put me in an ambulance and I was taken to the nearest hospital. I stayed in overnight then they released me, so I walked back to the camp and decided I would never try again. I called my uncle in Pakistan and told him it wasn't going to be easy getting to London as I had nearly lost my life. Hiding from the Taliban was bad, I said, but now I might die under a lorry so I was going to give up and would try and find somewhere to settle in France or Germany. I urged him not to pay the rest of the money to the traffickers because Mr Rana had guaranteed he would get me to the UK and far from getting special treatment paying $8,000, I was just like all the other illegals. My uncle told me not to try again and that he would speak to the traffickers who would send someone to find me.

They definitely wanted to get me to the UK otherwise they would have missed out on the final payment of our deal and each of the contacts along the way were getting paid. There were so many of them in the network, even in the UK; if you know what to look for they are easily recognisable because they all drive expensive cars but many of them are just apparently working in car washes. How can they afford BMWs and Mercedes doing that work? Today I work long hours but I cannot afford to buy a £10,000 car never mind £70,000. In the UK it is easy to become a millionaire if you are prepared to get involved in trafficking or drug dealing. This is the reality of what is going on every day and it is a global and well-organised network.

I waited another few days then a Kurdish man came to our camp searching for me. All the different nationalities – Afghans, Kurds, Iraqis – were grouped according to their countries with some even flying their national flags on their tents so it was relatively easy to track me down, asking for Nosher Khan. He explained that we could not just walk out of the camp together because he would be recognised by the Red Cross and reported to the police, so he told me to pack up my few belongings and walk 200 yards ahead of him back to the train station where he would meet me.

The following day I said goodbye to my friends saying I was giving up trying to get across the channel. I went back to the train station where the agent was waiting with two tickets and he took me all the way to Brussels. We went to a Turkish restaurant for a meal and he told me that, as I had a guarantee from Mr Rana, tomorrow I would be in the UK. I asked how he was going to do it because in Calais it was so difficult. All he said was it would be a surprise and I should finish my meal.

TEN

By lorry to England

A car was waiting outside the restaurant with a driver and another man in the front passenger seat, who had a handgun strapped to his waist. I was shocked. This might have been normal in Afghanistan but not in Europe. The agent told me to get in quickly, said goodbye and just slammed the door. Once again I was in the hands of complete strangers; I didn't know where we were going or how I would get to the UK. The men said nothing but raced away through the streets of Brussels; I don't think a word was spoken until we found ourselves driving at high speed down the motorway.

Suddenly the driver did an emergency stop and told me to jump out. We seemed to be in the middle of nowhere, but I realised it was pointless arguing. Once out of the car I stumbled down a steep embankment and found myself in a field of tall sweetcorn.

It was pitch dark and for a moment I thought I had been tricked but then I heard a voice calling: "Come, brother. Come." Then I saw what I assumed were two guides and another 16 people mostly Iraqi and Iranian and two or three Afghans: men, women and children among them. I guessed that they had all been waiting for me to arrive; I have no idea how long they must have been huddled together in that field but it would have been a terrifying experience for the children. Then we started walking through the fields of corn; I remember thinking why don't we pick some and cook them for a meal which is what we might have done during our long journey out of Afghanistan. We walked on for more than half an hour in single file in the darkness; we were not allowed to use a torch in case we were spotted by the police.

We eventually reached a lorry service station and one of our guides started checking the lorries, presumably to see which one was going to the UK, although I didn't know how he could tell. What I did begin to realise was how I was going to get to the UK – in the back of a container lorry.

The guide disappeared into the service station for five or ten minutes, then returned with a screwdriver and began opening the back door of one of the lorries, taking care not to damage the seals which would have been spotted by security at the border. He told us to get in but I remember checking to make sure that it was not a refrigerated container as I had been warned about them by the refugees in the camp; apart from the cold it would have made it difficult to breathe. Although it was a metal sided lorry, I could see that it was full of smart furniture and I knew it would be safe so climbed in.

Some people tried to hide behind the tables and chairs but I didn't bother because I thought if they stopped the lorry they would find us anyhow so what was the point. I sat next to an Arab lady with a two-year-old baby; it was screaming and her mother tried to calm her child down in case the noise attracted attention. A lot of the other refugees began shouting at her saying because of her child we would all be caught, but there was nothing she could do besides trying to rock the baby to sleep. The poor lady was crying too and I felt so sorry for her trying to cope all on her own; if it was a tough way to travel for me it must have been terrible for her.

I think it was a Polish lorry and I am sure the driver must have known we were in the back otherwise what was the agent doing in the service station – maybe he was paying off the driver – and where did he get the screwdriver?

The agents explained that we could talk as much as we liked once the lorry set off but after one and a half hours we had to be completely silent, not even a whisper and no coughing. For half an hour we were told we might feel some movement but that meant the lorry was on the train then everything would go dark, but there was no need to panic because we would be going through the Channel Tunnel. In fact there was not much talking when everyone had settled down into their own little corners. There was nothing to say; everyone knew the risk they were taking and for all of us this was probably the last leg in a long and dangerous journey. Either we were going to make it to the end or we would be sent home, but at least there was no danger of being shot by either European or British police.

We spent three or four hours in the lorry parked at the service station. I had some biscuits but no water and I was so thirsty. I began thinking what would we do if the lorry didn't move for two or three weeks. I wasn't worried about being caught because if we were we would be released anyway and I would be sent back to the Red Cross camp in Calais where I would be given food. My worry was what if we died inside the lorry because the lorry was parked in a corner somewhere and even if we shouted no one would hear us.

In the morning the lorry at last left for Calais driving all the way back through Belgium and France until we reached Calais. Some people had managed to sleep but I stayed awake huddled up against the cold.

When we got to the port we could hear dogs barking and we were sure the Border Agency people would find us again, but that danger passed. Then it got dark, just as they said as we passed through the tunnel, before we saw the sunshine through the lorry skylights. That was the signal for us to try and attract attention because we had been told that if we were stopped in the Dover port area we would have a much stronger case to claim asylum than if we were discovered further inland where the authorities might have suspected that we had been working illegally in the country for some time.

We immediately started trying to break through the skylights but they were made of tough plastic, so one of the migrants used two cigarette lighters to burn through the plastic before smashing it with a broken piece of furniture.

One man forced his way through the skylight and began waving his hands to attract attention. The lorry driver started speeding up because he did not want to be caught with us on board otherwise he would have been prosecuted and probably fined, but a motorist must have seen and called the police who stopped the lorry. When the two officers opened the door and saw all these people, they quickly slammed it shut again to prevent any of us running away and told the driver to turn round and go back to Dover.

There is a big detention centre in Dover. It looks like a vast white mountain but that is its only attraction; its purpose is to hold illegal immigrants like us and the unlucky ones are sent straight back to where they came from. The centre was crammed full with probably 200 or so other illegal immigrants.

News of our arrest quickly brought journalists and TV crews to see us and they asked if any of us spoke English and wanted to be interviewed. I put my hand up and said I had fled the fighting in Afghanistan, my life had been in danger and I hoped to build a new life in the UK, always remembering to keep my story simple and straightforward; it also happened to be true. I think news of 16 migrants being found in a container lorry was on the TV bulletins that night. But even before I had been formerly questioned, one of the immigration officers said I needn't worry. I was safe now as they were aware of the dangerous situation in Afghanistan and I would not be forced to return; I had a good chance of being granted asylum. A solicitor and interpreter were offered and we had our fingerprints taken, but that was the extent of our questioning although I think the lorry driver must have had a tougher interrogation. But at last I had reached the UK. It was 16 October 2001.

We were held in the detention centre overnight before being driven in a minibus to a hotel having been told that the Home Office would contact us later for a formal interview presumably to decide if we would be allowed to stay. But I saw a lot of Afghans being picked up by what I assumed were their relatives and just being driven away much to the relief of the UK Border Agency who otherwise would have had to find them accommodation while their cases were being reviewed. They wanted to get rid of us anyway. We were all given a letter granting us temporary permission to be in the UK.

The hotel was in Margate, Kent near the Dreamland Amusement Park and Entertainment Centre. It was where they housed all the asylum seekers for a week or two until they found them more permanent accommodation which might be in Birmingham, Manchester or Liverpool which were just some of the cities we heard about and all, of course, completely unknown to us. When I arrived at the hotel with about ten or 15 others, we all got allocated our rooms and were told not to go far because the immigration officials would come at any time to tell us which of these cities we were going to be sent to.

But there was no other restriction on our movements and I had a piece of paper which I could show to the police if I was stopped, so I decided to go for a walk. I saw a pizza shop near Dreamland where the staff looked like Afghan nationals. I thought I would see if I could get a job or if they could help me find a solicitor to get a visa.

The shop owner seemed very friendly and said he was looking for workers. He would also provide free accommodation above the shop so I wouldn't have to go to Birmingham or London where I would struggle because I didn't know anybody. My luck seemed to have changed at last.

I called two of my cousins living in Southall, London who immediately came down to see me and spent the night in my room above the pizza shop. They took my photo and promised to show it to my mom to prove that I had reached the UK safely. They didn't suggest I should go and live with them, and they warned me that life was tough in the UK. I would have to make a good case for my asylum if I wanted to stay otherwise I might be deported back to Afghanistan. They asked me if I had ever been finger printed while in mainland Europe and I said no which was just as well because if my prints had come up on a database in France or Belgium I would have been sent back there.

They advised me to stay where I was and learn how to make pizzas, then they went back to Southall. It didn't seem like much of a future and I was disappointed. I had no idea how to apply for a visa or find a solicitor and nobody from the border agency got in touch with me probably because I had left the hotel. When I told the hotel staff that I had found accommodation they were delighted – it simply freed up another room as far as they were concerned and I signed a piece of paper saying I was going freely and giving my new address.

I walked back to the pizza shop from the hotel and the owner then told me I had to sleep in a living room with three or four other staff because the rooms were no longer empty. It was a blow but I could do nothing about it even if most of the other staff were probably either illegal immigrants or working for "black money" and off the shop's books.

They kept me for about six or seven months with no wages, only free pizza and one can of Coca Cola a day. I had no idea of the law about minimum wages and I was just told I wasn't being paid because I was a trainee. I was also doing door-to-door leafleting but it was a cold, wet winter and my fingers turned blue as I walked the streets and I couldn't bend them. Every day I had to deliver 500 leaflets door to door so we got busy and then I was trained to make pizzas.

I asked one of the workers who I should speak to in order to apply for a visa and seek asylum because no one had contacted me from the Home Office even though I had given the hotel my new address. The pizza owner said I should talk to one of his family members, Mr Abdul Malik, who was acting as a case worker based in Wembley.

One of the other workers lent me £20 pounds for the train ticket which I promised to repay when I was given Home Office vouchers which I could exchange for cash or clothes.

I went to Wembley and found Malik's small office. In reality he didn't have a licence to operate and later I found out the Home Office closed his business down. I thought I had hit another dead end but Malik called me to say he had handed my case on to an Indian solicitor called Mr Raja who told me that in fact the Home Office had refused my asylum case because I had not given a proper interview and my application had just been handwritten. However, I had been granted a four-year visa after which, according to the law, my case would be reconsidered.

I decided not to appeal the decision because America was by then in Afghanistan and I reasoned that if the Taliban could take control of the country in six months then surely it would be easy for America to do it faster. In 2001, Hamid Karzai had been sworn in as head of a power sharing government, so hopefully in two years time I would be able to go back voluntarily to Afghanistan because I could see how much of a struggle life was going to be in the UK. I realised that I was in the UK but I was confident that America would be able to defeat the Taliban and Al Qaeda as well as the Mujahideen who the US were by then calling terrorists. My plan was to return to Afghanistan, find a job and make $8000 to repay my father. I would also be able to rebuild my home and be with my family once more.

The solicitor told me to have my photo taken and he gave me an ID card. He also gave me a Samsung mobile phone for free because he said he was making money from the Home Office for every asylum case he handled. He paid for me to have a takeaway lunch and told me I had to apply for a National Insurance number if I wanted to work.

I returned to Margate and quickly mastered all the names of the pizza toppings and slowly learned how to answer the phone, but still the owner didn't pay me a penny. I was struggling financially and I asked one of my colleagues why were other people being paid and I was not and he said it was up to the boss and advised me to leave because this was not the type of work I should be doing as I spoke several languages, had a little education and a skill as a TV engineer.

A possible new job came up near Ramsgate, Kent but I needed a National Insurance number which one of my colleagues said I could get from the job centre. After I finished my leafleting one morning I went straight to the nearest job centre where a lady took all my details and told me to wait. A big man came in and sat next to me but I noticed he was looking at me rather angrily; then he asked me where I was from. When I said Afghanistan he started shouting: "How dare you bloody immigrants come to this country, taking our money and our jobs." I tried to reason with him saying I had a job but I just needed a National Insurance number.

But I realised then for the first time that perhaps people were not happy with immigrants coming to the UK; the truth is I never thought about it from their perspective and all I was doing was fleeing from certain death and trying to earn my keep. It may be a fine distinction but there is a difference between refugee and immigrant, illegal or not. I may have got into the country by illegal means but I was a refugee; my life was in danger and would remain so if I returned to my home country. I came prepared to work and earn my keep and there was no other way I could have made it into any country in Europe.

The lady behind the counter heard the exchange and told the man not to speak to me like that and that I had every right to be there. I decided that this was the wrong place for me and stood up to leave. She tried to get me to wait and asked me what my birthday date was. I gave it to her but left anyway. A week later I received a letter with my

National Insurance card and she had given me the number to match the year I was born. I think she must have done it to make it easier for me to remember.

I was so happy now I could work legally and get out of the pizza shop. I asked people where I could find work repairing TVs and they said people don't repair them they just chuck them in the bin and buy a new one. I was amazed; people in the UK were so rich they didn't care. They just call their insurance company and get a new one. I thought I should collect all the broken TVs and send them to Afghanistan, but I was told I needed a special permit to move waste products and anyhow where would I store them. I gave up hoping to revive my old career.

ELEVEN

Job hunting, abuse and citizenship

Eventually I received my vouchers for cash and clothes. It was a huge book which seemed very generous to me as I had never been given such a free and valuable gift before. I didn't need all the clothes vouchers so I gave half of them to my friends in the pizza shop which they were surprised by and grateful for, but they had supported me and I was happy to share my good fortune with them.

This was my chance to break free and I told my boss that I was going to leave because he was not paying me and so I wanted to give in my notice. But he told me to wait because, as I was now trained, he would pay me £200 a week; however, he wanted me to work in another one of his shops in Tonbridge, Kent where there would be accommodation. I wasn't sure I could trust him but if at last I was going to be paid then it was worth the risk. I shouldn't have been so gullible. He told me to keep a record of all the shifts I worked and that he would pay me later.

He drove me all the way to his shop in Tonbridge which he said was so busy. He then took me to a house where I would be staying but as soon as I walked through the front door I saw a mass of bags and clothes everywhere. I discovered that 16 people were living in the same house which only had three bedrooms and a sitting room. I asked him where I was supposed to sleep and he told me to put my blanket on the floor in the sitting room and sleep there. I thought this was just like my life in a refugee camp only at least our tent was not this crowded; in fact I would say the refugee camp was better in some ways. There were 20 or 30 pairs of smelly shoes lined up and I thought: my God is this what living in the UK is like?

But I just accepted the situation and said I now had to sleep. Around midnight, when the shop closed, a whole bunch of people came into the house; some welcomed me, some ignored me. They didn't care that I was trying to sleep and they played music or watched the TV and chatted. I told them that I had a visa and National Insurance number and so I had no trouble with the police but they warned me that if anyone should knock on the door I mustn't answer it which seemed strange. They explained that about ten of the people staying in the house and working at the shop were illegal immigrants and the boss didn't want the council to know how many people were living in the house. I wondered what the neighbours thought about it and they said they had no trouble with them because they supplied them with free pizzas. I stayed in that living room for months.

The work again involved leafleting. I was given a bag of leaflets which had to be distributed in neighbouring towns like Sevenoaks, Hildenborough and Tunbridge Wells. My routine was going to the shop in the morning, counting out 500 leaflets then being dropped off by a pizza delivery van driver to do my rounds. The shop then opened at 11.30am and we began the process of making hundreds of pizzas. I used to make about 130 pizzas a day after finishing leafleting; we would have our lunch and then start another shift from 5pm to midnight and on Fridays and Saturdays until 3am. We had a short break and were allowed one medium pizza a day and a can of Coca Cola – we were treated like prisoners and slaves. I still hadn't been paid.

One day the manager whose job it was to answer the phone took me aside and told me that I shouldn't be working for what he called these evil people as I spoke several languages and had a training. I wondered why he had stuck at the job but he said he was being well paid; he was getting £400 a week. I asked if that was after tax and he just laughed saying we don't pay tax – it is all black money. I told him that was why English people hate us because we work and we don't pay taxes and I remembered the man in the job centre. I realised what he meant about immigrants coming to the country taking jobs and not paying taxes. It may not be the same in every fast food outlet but there is no doubt that many are bending the rules. What most of them do is when the shift ends if they are making £10,000 a week, the managers will print off another copy of the sales receipts and delete from the computer what is actually made. So at the end of the day if they actually made £1,000 the print out would show £200 for tax purposes. It is a very common practice.

I don't know what the other staff were doing but I saved what little money I was making. I walked everywhere, bought nothing and lived off pizzas. As always I thought there must be something better waiting for me round the corner and I suppose I was saving for that moment.

One day I said to my only friend, the manager, that I was not like the others who could barely speak English, I had some education although I didn't have any formal qualifications and I agreed with him that I didn't want to go on working like a slave. I asked him if he could help me find another job.

He sent me to Croydon where Samsung had a big warehouse fixing TVs but it was no good because, although I had the skills, I didn't have a degree and I could not start studying at that stage in my life, so at that point I gave up all hope of doing the job I liked and was trained for.

When I threatened to hand in my notice and leave the pizza shop the boss told me to collect all my belongings because he wanted to take me to another shop in Purley. He said I was his best pizza maker and he wanted me to build up the business there in return for £200 a week but I had to deliver leaflets seven days a week and make pizzas seven nights a week.

I asked for the wages I was owed from the Tonbridge shop and he said he would not run away and steal my money.

I started work in Purley for a few months but again I had to live in a crowded house with 15 other people in Thornton Heath which is nearly five miles away.

I really hated doing leaflets in Purley because so many of the properties involved going up and down stairs and I got so tired but I could not simply run away because my boss held all my wages. After a few months when he saw the Purley shop was getting busy, he asked me to work in another shop, this time in Sutton – but this involved leafleting in Purley and night shifts making pizzas in Sutton. It was a very hard situation for me. It was another five miles between Sutton and Purley and I still had to get back to Thornton Heath at the end of my shift. I had to travel by bus every day and was paid £10 a week for bus tickets.

One day I was so hungry that I bought a portion of chicken wings but forgot to keep some money back for my bus fare. I asked the manager to give me £2 for the bus but he refused because the boss had told him only to pay me £10 on a Monday and it was Sunday. I was too embarrassed to ask the other staff for the money and I decided to walk all the way from Purley to Sutton. I thought my God this is what life is like in the UK. It is worse than being homeless and I prayed to Allah for help.

Unbelievably I found a £20 note lying in the street soaking wet. At first I wondered if it was real or fake. I went to a shop to buy a can of coke to see if it was real because it was also the first time I had seen a £20 note. Luckily it was real and I was given my change.

After a few months working I got ill and an ambulance took me to hospital where I was diagnosed with a kidney problem. The doctor advised me to eat proper food and put on some more weight – I weighed exactly 41 kilograms or just over 6 stone.

I decided I had to give up working these long hours even if I didn't get my money back; I told the owner I was not feeling well and I wanted to go back to Tonbridge. He gave me about £500 cash.

My friendly manager said we both had to move out of the over-crowded house and he found a room to rent above an Indian restaurant in Southborough, a suburb of Tunbridge Wells. It was dark and had a dirty carpet but we cleaned it up and bought an extra bed for me from the Red Cross charity shop and walked with it all the way home through the streets. Everyone thought we were mad but we didn't think of hiring a van to transport the bed the few miles; we just stopped and rested every so often and then carried on. I was still working in the pizza shop walking the three miles from Southborough to Tonbridge every day.

At last, in 2003, my friend told me there was a job opportunity if I wanted to apply but I didn't know how to go about it. It was a big distribution centre for M&S in Tunbridge Wells which employed more than 600 people. With his help, we both applied and to my delight was called on my mobile for an interview the following Monday. My friend had also been called but his interview was the following day. I was worried because my English was poor and I had no idea what to expect or the questions I would be asked, but my friend said just say you are a very hard-working person.

At the interview I was asked a few questions which I didn't understand so I just kept nodding, but I remembered what my friend had told me and said I was a very hard-working man and would never let them down.

That seemed to be all they wanted to hear because I was immediately told I had passed the interview and asked if I could start the very next day; at that time there was a lot of demand for workers and no one seemed too concerned about where you came from or even if you had a work permit just as long as you were prepared to put in the hours.

I handed in my notice to the pizza shop owner who wasn't pleased. He said he had helped me get a visa by introducing me to his contact in Wembley and had trained me how to make pizzas. He didn't pay me anything for the six months I had been working for nothing in Margate and just threw me out.

The M&S distribution centre helped me apply for a Barclays bank account, which made me feel so proud. I thought at last my life was on track, my refugee status was a thing of the past and somehow I felt accepted.

My job was straightforward unloading clothes from lorries, scanning them and putting them on carousels and I was a very fast worker; my performance exceeded the 70% target I had been set and regularly hit 100%. My team leader was more than happy saying my performance was unbelievable, but I didn't want to lose my job so I was working hard.

But not everyone was so pleased. There were 13 bays and I was emptying the lorries in one hour but the other English workers were emptying half, taking a break and coming back to finish the job taking eight hours compared with my one hour. It wasn't long before they started hating me as I suppose I was showing them up. I simply had worked out how to scan the clothes faster than everyone else, which actually wasn't that difficult. But when I got back from my breaks I would find notes saying: Go back to your country.

I did have a few friends, a couple from New Zealand called Ron and Betty who were in their sixties and another friend from Thailand. They told me that English people were like that and hated immigrants, and advised me to show the notes to the manager but I just ignored the comments and threw them in the bin. I knew who was writing the notes, most of them female and they would sit around together gossiping in the canteen. It was a kind of jealousy, I suppose.

Every day I would listen to BBC Radio 2 news bulletins every half hour with stories from Afghanistan about British and American soldiers being killed; this was everyday news and then I heard there had been bombings in villages and Jalalabad itself. My colleagues, Ron and Betty, noticed that I was getting more and more depressed and I explained that my family were still in Afghanistan and I was worried that they might have been killed in the bombing because thousands of people had lost their lives during the fighting and I know that if the Taliban attacked Jalalabad airport they would definitely attack our village as it was so close.

In the meantime the company moved me from the hanging area to a different section because I was so strong. Now my job was emptying the lorries but the clothes were all too high up for me to reach the roof of the lorry which meant I had to jump to reach the top rows to hang the clothes on the carousels. So they got me some steps. Then the people who were doing the same work also turned against me because they were taking eight hours to empty one lorry while I was emptying two. It didn't take long for this news to spread through other departments and a friend told me that there was a lot of talk about a guy from Afghanistan who was breaking all the records.

Pride comes before a fall as they say and one day I did fall off the ladder and hurt my back badly enough that I had to be taken to hospital but I managed to carry on working. I tried to talk to the people who were against me in the canteen but they still refused to sit next to me.

In 2004, I noticed some new recruits from Eastern Europe had joined. Although I didn't speak Russian, Romanian or Lithuanian the company asked me to try and act as an interpreter and show them what to do instead of making me work on the lorries again because of my back and they also appreciated the fact that I hadn't claimed against the company for health and safety reasons which might have cost them thousands. I trained the people how to log in and scan my way, and the company moved all the English people to other departments because they wanted fast workers. In the process I met Anca, a girl from Romania and we became close; it was the first time in my life that I had had a girlfriend.

When I heard that Afghanistan was in fact getting worse day by day instead of better and I had no news about my family I got really stressed. It was getting close to the time when my visa was due to expire and my friends warned me that Afghanistan was never going to be the same as it was and I had to find another solicitor to apply for indefinite leave to stay in the UK because it would never be safe enough for me to return home even for a short holiday.

Tony Blair was still Prime Minister and David Blunkett was Home Secretary at the time and the law governing refugees was quite lax; according to the rules if you spent more than four years in the country you had the right to apply for indefinite leave to remain. I applied through my solicitor and after two weeks I was granted leave to stay, so now I was able to go to Pakistan to find my family knowing that I would be able to return to the UK.

In 2005 an announcement was made over the tannoy that all workers had to gather for a meeting. I thought it might be like Christmas when we were given wine and presents; I used to give my wine to the people who hated me saying I was a Muslim and didn't drink. They were taken aback by my gesture and I said all I asked is that they stopped writing rude notes to me. They apologised and slowly they became friends and even sat next to me in the canteen asking what news I had from my family in Afghanistan.

But the news our boss, Peter Smith, had for us over the loudspeaker was bad. He announced that in two weeks the warehouse would be closing down – not only ours but three others in the country. Distribution to M&S outlets was now to be handled by a company in Turkey where they were paying their workers £1 an hour. It was devastating news particularly for the likes of Ron and Betty who were approaching retirement.

A few days later I saw recruitment stands had been set up in the car park by a lot of different companies who were desperate for labour.

One of those was a firm looking for drivers. I had a driving licence and they offered me work for £500 a week. I was given the keys to a car and started work immediately. It was now 2005 and my luck had changed again.

If my career was becoming more stable my personal life was not and that was as a direct result of what I had been through. My girlfriend, Anca, and I had been together for a few years. I had rented a better room, but again the Pakistani landlord had also given rooms to six other people, plus us. This illegal letting is commonplace in the UK and probably elsewhere but it was an improvement on a blanket on the floor.

The fighting continued in Afghanistan and I was worrying about my family so I told Anca that I planned to return to Pakistan now I was free to re-enter the UK legally, but she didn't believe I would come back. I tried to reassure her pointing out that I had helped apply for her own asylum when she too had entered the UK in the back of a lorry claiming she had been forced into prostitution by her family. The Home Office accepted her case and gave her a visa.

In the end I went to Pakistan and found my aunt's house. They were surprised to see me but very happy particularly as I had brought some simple gifts which they would never have been able to buy in Peshawar. However, they had no news of my family and when I suggested sending my aunt's son they said that would be too risky because the Taliban were still everywhere. Pakistan was sending a lot of fighters to join them in Afghanistan and my aunt said she didn't even let her son go to the mosque in case he was brainwashed by the mullahs.

It was out of the question that I should go myself because I would be recognised in our village and probably betrayed to the Taliban once again, and this time there would have been no mercy. I went to the mosque regularly but all the preaching was about *jihad* and recruiting young men to fight against America with the Taliban in Afghanistan. Nothing had changed then and it probably remains the same today. The police did not seem to have any power and my aunt's husband, General Rafe, said this was exactly what Pakistan wanted. The last thing they needed on their border was a stable Afghanistan with a strong government as it would definitely lay claim to the long disputed Durand Line territory between the two countries established by the British in

1893. General Rafe said that America was now trying to destroy the Mujahideen who were once their allies fighting against the Russians and that was why America could not be trusted. It was a difficult time.

I spent one and a half months in Pakistan and returned to the UK still stressful. In 2006 I got a call on my mobile from my aunt who told me that my family were fine but she didn't tell me the truth.

In June that year my brother, Nur, suddenly turned up in the UK. He was wearing a big jumper and despite only being 15 looked much older with a long beard. The Home Office called me when I was dropping a passenger off at Heathrow to ask if I knew someone called Nur Mohammed. I said yes he was my brother but I thought he was still in Afghanistan. They said no he was being held at Bath police station 150 miles away. When I arrived, smartly dressed wearing a tie and clean shaven, they didn't believe that Nur, who was a bit fat, wrapped in a jumper with a full beard, was actually much younger than me. They thought he was lying about his age so that they wouldn't deport him back to Afghanistan because they couldn't deport children. In the end they believed me and I drove back to Tunbridge Wells and he moved in with me and my girlfriend, but she was not happy. I said I had no choice; he was my brother and told her I could find another girlfriend but not another brother so she moved out and went to stay with her sister.

I, of course, asked Nur how he came to be in the UK and how he made the journey. He refused to answer directly only saying that our father had made a mistake, which only worried me more.

In 2007 I was finally granted full British citizenship and as soon as Anca received her British passport she started to change – I think she was just using me and slowly the excuses started. She would say I am a Muslim and she was a Christian and her parents would never allow her to marry me. I tried to get her to change her mind saying I would look for a two-bedroom house which luckily I found through the local council and which meant my brother, Nur, had his own room. That worked for a time and Anca was happy. Then she started making comments that all Muslims were terrorists but I told her she didn't know what she was talking about – the fighting had nothing to do with what the Koran teaches. In fact I said if I were a good Muslim I shouldn't even be living with her but I wanted to marry her and make our relationship legal.

She invited her parents to meet me and although they could not speak a single word of English, they seemed to like me. I took them and Anca's sister who acted as an interpreter to an Afghan restaurant in London in my car and treated them like special guests. The mother said she didn't have a problem with me and was quite happy for me to marry her daughter. I said if her daughter was not happy I was not going to force her and so we broke up which was another stressful situation as I was alone again.

I decided that I had to go back to Pakistan and this time I would not return until I had found my family. I gave $2,000 to one of my relatives and asked them to bring my parents, and my two sisters back to Pakistan and I rented a house for them in Peshawar.

My mother said she wanted to see me get married and have children but she was shocked to learn that I had had a girlfriend and we had been living together. But I reassured her that now we had broken up.

Relieved, my mother said I had three cousins and I had to marry one of them. But this was asking a lot. I explained that I was living in the UK now and I was not going to accept an arranged marriage even if it was the tradition in our Afghan culture. But my mom piled on the pressure saying it was also in our culture not to go against the wishes of the family and that she had suffered a great deal bringing up all her children. I asked her to give me time and not force me which she agreed to but added that if I refused she would consider that she had lost a son. I promised to try and talk Anca round and see if she would convert to Islam which my mom regarded as absolution for my sins!

I told Anca that we had been together for three years but I could not force her to convert; however, if we had children we could let them decide if they wanted to be Christian or Muslim. If she didn't agree then I warned her that my mom would choose another wife for me.

Anca was not convinced. She said she was sure that I would marry her and then go back to Pakistan and marry a second wife as Muslims do. She said she didn't want her children to speak my language or be Muslim, so I said in that case we had to say goodbye forever.

I couldn't break my mom's heart so I called her and said I had to come and choose a wife from among my cousins but I told her that although she may think that was good news she was really breaking my heart not hers. Some people say you often have two options in life: jump into the fire or jump into the water. At least if you jump into the water you have a chance of swimming for your life and I was worried because I had heard about young girls being taken by their parents supposedly on holiday only to find they were about to be married off to a complete stranger.

My mom told me not worry because from the day she and my father married he had never once said: I love you. In time, she said, I would get used to my bride and I would definitely choose the pretty one.

I went to one cousin's house. The parents knew I lived in the UK and they thought that must mean I was a very rich man so I was invited as a guest for a meal and the girl helped serve the food but she was not even allowed to sit next to me even though we were cousins; in effect I had just a few seconds to make my mind. I didn't like the first two cousins I met.

Then I went to another house and saw another cousin who was the prettiest with blue eyes and I said to my mom that I would accept this girl. Then it was up to the girl's father to give his approval of me but he refused because his elder daughter was not yet married and I would have to wait until she found a husband.

I had returned to the UK to await the father's decision but when I heard that he had refused I told my mom that this was fate and she should let me try and find a wife in the usual way in the UK. But my mom was made of sterner stuff and refused to give up. She went again to see the family, this time with Nur who said he wanted to marry the older daughter, which seemed to solve all the problems. I asked Nur if he had made his decision just to help me and he said no.

Fatima and I married on 16 November 2006 in Pakistan where my daughter was born. I agreed to sponsor them both and they arrived in the UK in 2008. Now we have one daughter and three sons living a normal, some might say a mundane life but it is safer that way. Afghanistan is never far from my mind as I watch the news of the latest bombing and shooting every day. It seems absolutely nothing has changed since my family and I walked out of Kushgumbad that night all those years ago. We weren't the first refugees and we won't be the last to flee that country.

Epilogue

In 2003 Nato took control of security in Kabul which was its first operational role outside Europe and to those ordinary people in Afghanistan, in other words the majority who were not directly involved in any of the fighting, it probably seemed like a hopeful moment. Order would be restored, the warring factions of the Taliban, Al Qaeda, ISIL, the Mujahideen and President Hamid Karzai's government would be pushed to the sidelines and the country could return to its long forgotten peaceful existence, free from invaders and even free from those who came offering treaties which always seemed to benefit others.

At least that is how it may have looked to my father and he decided that he would take the opportunity to seek some justice for what had happened to his family. He wanted to complain personally to the governor of Jalalabad. So he travelled there to demand the return of the $3,000 bribe he had had to pay for my release from captivity by the Taliban; after all, they must surely have been driven out. But what he found was the same Taliban guards, this time masquerading as officials in smart suits and neatly trimmed beards. Same donkey, different clothes as he would say.

Of course, he was told firmly to go away as those matters were all in the past. But they weren't because a few days later three gunmen drove into Kushgumbad and asked where our home was. Someone I assume pointed it out and they saw my brother, Ahmed, playing outside. They immediately snatched him, put him in their car and drove away. They didn't say anything at the time and didn't even come into our house. We didn't even know if he was alive or dead. A few weeks later a note was left at our home warning my father to keep his mouth shut and not to complain about what had happened because they knew where to find him and furthermore they demanded another $8,000 for Ahmed's release. And that was the last we heard of him for three years. This was the mistake my father had made which Nur had been referring to.

It was all too much for Nur himself who, fearing that he would also be taken, ran away. He was just 13 years old. He followed my route catching a bus to Jalalabad – children don't have to pay – and travelled through Iran until he finally reached Peshawar where he went to look for my aunt. Eventually he told me the full story of how he had escaped from Afghanistan and reached the UK.

In fact the whole process took him three years because, as he explained to me, he had met up with a group of Hazara people when he first reached Iran and decided to join them because he had no other friends. They began work on a construction site where they stayed for six or seven months; he was given free food but very little money because his employers said that they were saving the rest up for him for when he went back to his own country. But they didn't pay him so he took some money from the office and he and three others ran away.

Then, like me, they met some human traffickers; they are so easy to find in Afghanistan, Pakistan and even in the UK, so long as you know what to look out for. If someone wanted to reach Canada from the UK without the right paperwork, for example, it would cost £15,000 and they would travel by air as easily as a regular passenger.

By chance Nur had met another cousin of the same age while he was in Iran, both still about 14 years old, and they decided that they would try and reach Turkey. So little by little they managed to get enough money to pay the human traffickers who took them all the way to the Turkish border; on the way they got caught in heavy snow and were forced to eat leaves to survive. At one stage they were stopped by Turkish Kurds who beat them and searched through their belongings demanding money but, of course, they didn't have anything worth taking and said they were just poor refugees who had escaped from Afghanistan.

Eventually they reached Istanbul, walking the whole way, sleeping outside in the dark. They were not alone as every night they saw more people crossing the border; nothing will stop this stream of migration so long as there is fighting or hunger, or both and it doesn't matter where that is happening in the world. When you are desperate or frightened for your life you will risk everything.

Despite the fact that they couldn't speak any Turkish, they managed to find work making shoes in a factory just by repeating the word: Work, Work. Needless to say the factory owners didn't care that the boys were just children because they needed workers. Exploitation of the vulnerable is also commonplace and, again, it is not restricted to underdeveloped societies; the slave trade is thriving behind closed doors in the civilised West.

Having saved up a little money, Nur found some other human traffickers to get him from Turkey to Greece. This was the riskiest part of the journey because he was put in an inflatable boat designed for eight but with 14 other people. The sight of refugees clinging to overloaded craft is almost a daily occurrence, and just as common is the sight of bodies being recovered from the seas. But Nur was lucky because they were spotted by the Greek authorities, rescued and put in a camp where he didn't stay for long because he smuggled himself onto a big ship bound for Italy. There, he made his way to a station and somehow managed to avoid ticket collectors until the train reached Calais.

Finally in June 2006 he hid under a lorry on the chassis. Immigration control didn't spot him or his friend who was hiding alongside him and they clung on while the driver drove all the way from Dover to Bath until he stopped in a service station. The two boys, their faces covered in grease and oil, then started walking along the motorway where inevitably they were picked up by a police patrol car.

Although the police believed we were brothers when I finally reached Bath, the issue about Nur's real age proved to be a greater problem. He was initially refused asylum status and I had to go to court to prove that he was indeed my younger 15-year-old brother. Again at the first hearing his case was rejected; they thought he was lying as young children cannot be deported. But he had the right to appeal and I was called as a witness. I got the judge to ask the immigration officer's barrister to check all the Afghan cases he was handling to see who gave their proper age. I took out my driving licence which stated that I was born on 1 January 1979 and the judge said I was very lucky to have been born on New Year's Day, which would have made my mother laugh given her own thoughts about her "unlucky child". I told him that I didn't really know which day I was born but I did know that Nur was born in 1991. I was also sure the barrister would confirm that most of the Afghan cases he was handling would show that the individuals were claiming to be born on 1 January. In fact when police stop people and their paperwork shows that they were born on 1 January they would immediately say: "You must be an Afghan", it was that well known. The judge immediately dismissed the case and granted Nur refugee status.

Just as I had done years earlier, he began work in a pizza shop in Maidstone, Kent putting in long hours trying to save money. He met some fellow Afghans who told him he should learn to relax a little and join them playing cricket which he did and later joined another club when he moved to be nearer to me in Tunbridge Wells and got other Afghans and some Pakistanis to join. Every Sunday, Nur, who is a good cook, prepared lunch for the other players and he was settling in to the local community well when he heard that the cricket ground was to be handed over to a football club by the local council. Nur decided that he and his fellow players should fight the decision and, when they managed to win a county final tournament, the club was given a reprieve.

For years, however, there was no news of our brother, Ahmed, who had been kidnapped by the Taliban and we all assumed that he must have been killed; it was quite normal for the Taliban to snatch children and sometimes cut off their captives' fingers or ears and demand a ransom for their release. If the families didn't agree the children would usually be killed.

What had happened to Ahmed was the NATO bombardment had become so heavy that the Taliban, along with their hostages, had kept moving, hiding in the mountainside and sheltering in different provinces; much of the time he had no idea where he was. Initially he had been tied up in case he ran away, but then they forced him to fight alongside them and trained him how to use a Kalashnikov; eventually he became skilled at stripping down the guns and reassembling them. It was either fight with them or be killed – he had no real choice.

In the end, after three years, they were caught by fighters from General Rashid Dostum's Northern Alliance. General Dostum became Vice President of Afghanistan in 2014 but in the country's long history he has fought for the Afghan National Army and has been both for and against the Mujahideen.

Ahmed and the other prisoners were all questioned but as soon as Ahmed started speaking Farsi they asked him if he was from Kabul and he explained that he had been captured from his village outside Jalalabad. One of the militia from Dostum's forces asked how come he spoke Farsi and Ahmed said that his mother came from Mazar-i-Sharif where the dominant language is Farsi. Immediately they said they were from Mazar-i-Sharif as well and pulled him aside to line up with a different group of prisoners away from the Taliban.

He was lucky because they then started beating the other Taliban prisoners trying to get information out of them – they had a list of names of people they were trying to find. One of the prisoners was hit so hard that he died and they simply pushed him down the mountain. The Taliban have kidnapped so many women and children, but General Dostum's forces were also accused of war crimes including the suffocation and shooting of 2,000 prisoners in December 2001 – accusations he denied.

Dostum's men drove Ahmed and some of the other captives to Mazar-i-Sharif where they were released. Ahmed was keen to get back to Jalalabad but he was warned that that was too dangerous so, with no money and no job, he was reduced to begging outside one of the mosques but even that was hopeless as no one seemed to want to give money or food to the beggar in dirty clothes and no shoes on his feet.

He started walking the streets and eventually found a master tailor where he offered his services. It must have been quite a sight: a tramp in rags claiming to be a skilled tailor. But it didn't take long for Ahmed to demonstrate the technique and ability he had learned, and not only did the owner offer him a job, but over time came to regard him as his own son. One day the shop owner said Ahmed should marry one of the many orphaned girls of the town who had lost their parents in the fighting. Apparently unaware that his own family were wondering if he was alive or dead, Ahmed married and settled down to life in Mazar-i-Sharif. But we were worried; most of the family were convinced he had been killed because no ransom had been paid but our mom believed that he was still alive somewhere. It had all proved too much for my father who had had a heart attack and died.

I went to the Red Cross in London with Ahmed's picture and told them his story. They tried checking with their contacts in Afghanistan and Pakistan but they could find no trace of him. I told my mom and tried to persuade her to come back to live in the UK with me; she was elderly and suffering from diabetes. But she said she was too frail to travel and, more importantly, she had had a dream that a child of hers was calling her and she didn't want to leave Pakistan in case Ahmed came looking for her.

Someone in Mazar-i-Sharif met Ahmed who told him his remarkable story and by chance that man travelled to Jalalabad and recounted the story to a man who knew our family. We told mom the good news that Ahmed was alive and, without saying a word to me, she took a bus back to Afghanistan with my younger brother, Faiz, and began searching for him. By night they stayed in a mosque and by day they walked the streets trying every tailor's shop they could find without success.

When I heard what they had done, I went back to the Red Cross to see if they could try again but they held out no hope. I decided to send my brother and a friend back to Afghanistan, gave them some money and told them to try again. After two weeks they found him. They all headed to Jalalabad and from there they made their way back to Pakistan where they all live together in Peshawar.

Towards the end of 2019, President Trump reopened peace talks with the Taliban, a hostage release was arranged to smooth the negotiations and pressure was put on the Taliban to honour a ceasefire. On 29 February 2020 an agreement was signed in Doha by Washington's representative, Zakmay Khalilzad, and Mullah Barada for the Taliban and immediately the Taliban declared the signing as a day of victory and Taliban supporters marched through the Qatari capital in celebration. In August 2020 the Taliban pushed harder and insisted the final 400 hard line fighters should also be released. The Afghan grand assembly, the Loya Jirga, agreed that this last stumbling block to peace was acceptable.[1] But what had any of this to do with the ordinary people of Afghanistan? Assuming all the terms of the deal stick, which is a big assumption, the Taliban are free to impose strict Sharia law, in the country, a law which is entirely alien to Afghans?

I understand that America wanted to get out of the country after almost 20 years and a cost of some $1 trillion and wash its hands of

---

1 *BBC*, 9 August 2020

the whole disastrous and failed campaign, longer than America's involvement in the First World War, the Second World War and the Vietnam War all put together. But what is it leaving behind? It will be a country controlled by the very organisation bent on the destruction of Western ideals it sought to impose, a training ground for terrorism. It will be a country which pollutes the world with opium production and, if ISIL's caliphate taught us anything, it is that the Taliban will not turn its back on such a lucrative trade. In December 2019 the Washington Post published 2,000 pages of confidential interviews quoting, among others, US General Douglas Lute as saying: "We didn't have the foggiest notion of what we were undertaking." A study of history would have told them of the perils of fighting in Afghanistan. Why don't people put pressure on Pakistan to stop supporting the Taliban? There is a lot of hatred for Taliban in Afghanistan and yet many of the Taliban are Afghans. The ordinary Afghan Muslim peasant is the only loser and they suffer the most.

In August 2021, Kabul airport became a chaotic staging post with thousands of terrified families fleeing for their lives seeking, like me, a better and safer life. The numbers will only increase with a secure Taliban government free to develop its own caliphate in my home country. And although I am lucky enough to be called a British citizen and one who has enjoyed the privileges of a safe and prosperous country for which I will always be grateful, if I had a choice I would give all that up tomorrow to return to the simple life of an Afghan farmer, tending my cattle and growing my vegetables. I know that is all a dream because I would be killed the day I set foot back in the country by a vengeful regime and, of course, my own young, British family would never be able to cope with the hardship of a simple life with no electricity or running water. But it is not just a question of what would happen to me; my sadness is what will happen to Afghanistan when the West walks away.

It seems that no one ever wins in Afghanistan – the British were driven out, the Russians were humiliated and in 2021 America brought an end to its futile struggle. The Afghan people, of course, never win but then again they are never wholly defeated. Their spirit will be crushed for a time, maybe years, under the cruel Taliban regime, who will seek to export both terrorism and drugs to the Western world, despite their assurances, but somehow Afghans always recover. And which country will dare to take on the challenge to fight the Taliban? A resurgent, but weakened Mujahideen will try to push back and may even ask for outside help. But then the circle of violence returns just as it did when America asked Pakistan to act as a go-between to arm Mujahideen fighters against the Russians only for General Zia to cut a deal with his favourites among the Peshawar Seven, ultimately releasing powerful weapons into the hands of separate factions each one carving out its own sphere of influence within a fractured country.

Afghanistan is both cursed and blessed by its natural resources and its geography so it cannot simply be left alone by outsiders because there is too much at stake. But equally is it too much for individuals to be left alone to follow their own way of simple life or even their own faiths? The answer is probably yes because essentially there is money to be made and someone will always want to make more. The traffickers who moved me across continents did it for money as people traffickers continue to do because so many people are so desperate; someone will always be ready to exploit the vulnerable, refugees and illegal migrants, as happened to me when I reached the West, because those migrants cannot answer back; and the drug traffickers will always export their poison because countless millions are prepared to beg, borrow and steal to pay for their next hit. The villagers of Kushgumbad understood this as they traded their cannabis to the eager Russians in Jalalabad airport, but does that make them culpable or simply desperate? Same donkey, different clothes.

Afghans themselves are not blameless in what has descended into fighting between rival militia warlords defending their own territories against each other and against the Afghan government forces. Corruption is rife and the prospects of finding lasting peace in the country look remote while the turf wars continue because as usual there is too much at stake. And throughout the land in madrassas, young minds are being poisoned about the benefits of *jihad* and encouraged to pick up an AK47 and practise how to use it for when they are old enough. They have learned nothing about science or literature, but they have become proficient killers before their graduation.

Perhaps the utter senselessness of all the violence in Afghanistan is best summed up by the death of the Japanese doctor, Tetsu Nakamura, in December 2019. He had devoted his life to improving the lives of all Afghans. He was shot dead by unnamed gunmen in Jalalabad on his way to work which involved the construction of wells and irrigation to villages where people were suffering from cholera because of the lack of clean water. I didn't cry when some of my relatives died, but I did cry when I heard of Dr Nakamura's death.

In 2002, when Jack Straw, the British Foreign Secretary, told the House of Commons that he expected British Forces to be home by Christmas, I did not appeal to the court against the Home Office for initially refusing my asylum case. I thought that if the fighting was over I would volunteer to go back to Afghanistan. But in 2020, as the 19th Christmas was approaching, the war in Afghanistan looked like it would last forever. The Taliban were driving a hard bargain for the release of their captive fighters; there was a weak Afghan government and US presidential elections were fast approaching in November which placed Trump under pressure to bring an end to American troops on the ground. As for civilians, anyone with a link, however tenuous, to President Ghani's rule, even interpreters working for the Americans, knew they would be a target for revenge should the Taliban ever take over. While the fragile peace talks stuttered into life in mid-2020 the killing continued with both the Taliban and IS admitting responsibility for atrocities: a mosque was bombed, a maternity ward riddled with bullets and soldiers of the Afghan army must have wondered whether they would be safer if they deserted and changed sides.

Instead of being a farmer in Afghanistan or even a shoe shine boy, I am a driver in the UK without influence, but I have eyes and some firsthand experience of what can happen to a vulnerable country which everyone wants to govern. It always ends in conflict and that always means that people will want to escape in search of a little peace and a little prosperity. The illegal migrants will continue to flood across borders and we can be certain that the only exports from a country at war will be terrorism because someone has to be blamed. Is it the drug addicts or the drug dealers feeding their habit which has now turned Europe itself into the cocaine hub of the world exporting to Australia, Turkey and Russia?

When I fled from Afghanistan with my family that dark night in 1985, I at least was full of hope. Anything had to be better than the mud brick walls of our home without power or running water. But I now realise that I was just fleeing from one battle to another. The drug pushers in the West simply drive smarter cars than the farmers in the poppy fields at home; those who brought terror to my shop stabbing me in the head, are replicated by knife-wielding *jihadists* on the streets of London; and those who call for peace are still prepared to make deals with anyone without any apparent thought as to the consequences, just as those who thought it wise to sell Stinger missiles as one way of defeating the Russian invaders gave little thought to what was likely to follow.

Same donkey, different clothes.